_To_

From

Date

365 DAILY DEVOTIONS

A
WOMAN'S
Garden
of
FAITH,
HOPE, &
LOVE

The quoted ideas expressed in this book (but not Scripture verses) are not, in all cases, exact quotations, as some have been edited for clarity and brevity. In all cases, the author has attempted to maintain the speaker's original intent. In some cases, quoted material for this book was obtained from secondary sources, primarily print media. While every effort was made to ensure the accuracy of these sources, the accuracy cannot be guaranteed. For additions, deletions, corrections, or clarifications in future editions of this text, please write Freeman-Smith, LLC.

Scripture quotations are taken from:

Scriptures marked NIV° are from the Holy Bible, New International Version°. Copyright © 1973, 1978, 1984 by International Bible Society. Used by permission of Zondervan Publishing House. All rights reserved.

Scriptures marked NASB are taken from the New American Standard Bible°. © Copyright The Lockman Foundation 1960, 1962, 1963, 1968, 1971, 1972, 1973, 1975, 1977, 1995. Used by permission. (www.Lockman.org).

Scriptures marked NKJV are taken from the New King James Version°. Copyright © 1982 by Thomas Nelson, Inc. Used by permission. All rights reserved.

Scriptures marked NLT are taken from the Holy Bible, New Living Translation, copyright © 1996. Used by permission of Tyndale House Publishers, Inc., Wheaton, Illinois 60189. All rights reserved.

Scriptures marked NCV are quoted from The Holy Bible, New Century Version, copyright © 1987, 1988, 1991 by Word Publishing, Nashville, TN 37214. Used by permission.

Scriptures marked KJV are taken from the King James Version.

Scripture quotations marked MSG are taken from The Message. Copyright © by Eugene H. Peterson 1993, 1994, 1995. Used by permission of NavPress Publishing Group.

Scripture quotations marked ICB are taken from the International Children's Bible, New Century Version © 1986, 1988 by Word Publishing, Nashville, TN 37214. Used by permission.

Scripture quotations marked TLB are taken from The Living Bible copyright © 1971. Used by permission of Tyndale House Publishers, Inc., Wheaton, Illinois 60189. All rights reserved.

Scripture quotations marked HCSB are taken from the Holman Christian Standard Bible °, Copyright © 1999, 2000, 2002, 2003 by Holman Bible Publishers. Used by permission. Holman Christian Standard Bible°, Holman CSB°, and HCSB° are federally registered trademarks of Holman Bible Publishers.

Cover Design by Kim Russell / Wahoo Designs
Page Layout by Bart Dawson

ISBN 978-1-58334-501-6

Printed in the United States of America

365 DAILY DEVOTIONS

A
WOMAN'S
Garden
of
FAITH,
HOPE, &
LOVE

Introduction

The dictionary defines the word garden as "a plot of land used to grow flowers, fruits, or vegetables." This definition is correct, as far as it goes. But those of us who carefully cultivate our own little plots of God's good earth know that a garden is much more than a place for growing plants. It is also a place to renew our spirits as we commune with our Creator and marvel at the beauty of His creation.

Faith, hope, and love are emotions that, like a garden, can be cultivated or neglected. When we nurture our faith through prayer, meditation, and worship, God enriches our lives and lifts our spirits. And this book is intended to help. This text is a collection of 365 spirit-lifting devotional messages that can help you cultivate your own "garden of faith, hope, and love." When you do, you will reap a rich harvest of spiritual blessings and a cornucopia of earthly rewards.

A garden can be an island of sanity amid the pressures and demands of modern-day living. But many of us lack the opportunity or the time to sink our spades into the soil. This book, while no substitute for the garden, is intended to provide similar comforts and pleasures.

As you consider the ideas on these pages, remember that faith, hope, and love, like tender seedlings, must be nurtured and protected. And remember that the most important seed you'll ever plant is the seed of Christ's love that you plant forever in your heart.

The Garden of Your Soul

Remember this: the person who sows sparingly will also reap sparingly, and the person who sows generously will also reap generously.

2 Corinthians 9:6 HCSB

Our hearts are like gardens that can be nurtured or neglected. If we leave our hopes untended— or if we contaminate them with the twin poisons of discouragement and doubt—the gardens of our souls produce few fruits. But, if we nurture our hopes through a firm faith in God and a realistic faith in ourselves, we bring forth bountiful harvests that bless us, our families, and generations yet unborn.

If the garden of your soul has been overtaken by the negativity that is an unfortunate hallmark of the age in which we live, don't be discouraged. Simply turn your thoughts and prayers to the Father and to the Son. Then trust in God's promises. And finally, make the resolution to tend your spiritual garden every day that you live. A garden is a lovely place to visit if it is tended with care, so cultivate yours carefully, and then reap the bountiful harvest that God has in store for you.

"They that sow bountifully shall reap also bountifully," is as true in spiritual things as in material.

Lottie Moon

The Abundant Life

A thief comes to steal and kill and destroy, but I came to give life—life in all its fullness.

John 10:10 NCV

When Jesus talks of the abundant life, is He talking about material riches or earthly fame? Hardly. The Son of God came to this world, not to give it prosperity, but to give it salvation. Thankfully for Christians, our Savior's abundance is both spiritual and eternal; it never falters—even if we do—and it never dies. We need only to open our hearts to Him, and His grace becomes ours.

God's gifts are available to all, but they are not guaranteed; those gifts must be claimed by those who choose to follow Christ. As believers, we are free to accept God's gifts, or not; that choice, and the consequences that result from it, are ours and ours alone.

As we go about our daily lives, may we accept God's promise of spiritual abundance, and may we share it with a world in desperate need of the Master's healing touch.

The gift of God is eternal life, spiritual life, abundant life through faith in Jesus Christ, the Living Word of God.

Anne Graham Lotz

To Study or Not to Study?

Jesus answered, "It is written: 'Man does not live by bread alone, but on every word that comes from the mouth of God.'"

MATTHEW 4:4 NIV

If you really want to know God, you should read the book He wrote. It's called the Bible, and it is one of the most important tools that God uses to direct your steps and transform your life.

As you seek to build a deeper relationship with your Creator, you must decide whether God's Word will be a bright spotlight that guides your path every day or a tiny nightlight that occasionally flickers in the dark. The decision to study the Bible—or not—is yours and yours alone. But make no mistake: the way that you choose to use your Bible will have a profound impact on you and your loved ones.

Your Bible is waiting patiently on your bookshelf . . . now, what are you going to do about it?

Study the Bible and observe how the persons behaved and how God dealt with them. There is explicit teaching on every condition of life.

CORRIE TEN BOOM

He Rewards Integrity

The integrity of the upright guides them, but the unfaithful are destroyed by their duplicity.

PROVERBS 11:3 NIV

The Bible makes it clear that God rewards integrity just as surely as He punishes duplicity. So, if we seek to earn the kind of lasting rewards that God bestows upon those who obey His commandments, we must make honesty the hallmark of our dealings with others.

Character is built slowly over a lifetime. Character is the sum of every right decision, every honest word, every noble thought, and every heartfelt prayer. It is built upon a foundation of industry, generosity, and humility. Character is a precious thing—difficult to build but easy to tear down. As believers in Christ, we must seek to live each day with discipline, honesty, and faith. When we do, integrity becomes a habit. And God smiles.

Sow an act, and you reap a habit. Sow a habit and you reap a character. Sow a character and you reap a destiny.

ANONYMOUS

Real Contentment

I have learned to be content in whatever circumstances I am.

PHILIPPIANS 4:11 HCSB

Where can you find contentment? Is it a result of wealth, or power, or beauty, or fame? Hardly. Genuine contentment springs from a peaceful spirit, a clear conscience, and a loving heart (like yours!).

Our modern world seems preoccupied with the search for happiness. We are bombarded with messages telling us that happiness depends upon the acquisition of material possessions. These messages are false. Enduring peace is not the result of our acquisitions; it is the inevitable result of our dispositions. If we don't find contentment within ourselves, we will never find it outside ourselves.

Thus the search for content is an internal quest, an exploration of the heart, mind, and soul. You can find contentment—indeed you will find it—if you simply look in the right places. And the best time to start looking in those places is now.

Those who are God's without reserve are, in every sense, content.

HANNAH WHITALL SMITH

If You Become Discouraged

Do not be afraid or discouraged, for the LORD is the one who goes before you. He will be with you; he will neither fail you nor forsake you.

DEUTERONOMY 31:8 NLT

Even the most devout Christians can become discouraged, and you are no exception. After all, you live in a world where expectations can be high and demands can be even higher.

If you find yourself enduring difficult circumstances, don't lose hope. If you face uncertainties about the future, don't become anxious. And if you become discouraged with the direction of your day or your life, don't despair. Instead, lift your thoughts and prayers to your Heavenly Father. He is a God of possibility, not negativity. You can be sure that He will guide you through your difficulties and beyond them . . . far beyond.

The most profane word we use is "hopeless." When you say a situation or person is hopeless, you are slamming the door in the face of God.

KATHY TROCCOLI

Strength for Today

*Those who hope in the LORD will renew their strength.
They will soar on wings like eagles; they will run and not
grow weary, they will walk and not be faint.*

ISAIAH 40:31 NIV

All of us have moments when we feel drained. All of us suffer through difficult days, trying times, and perplexing periods of our lives. Thankfully, God stands ready and willing to give us comfort and strength if we turn to Him.

If you're a woman with too many demands and too few hours in which to meet them, don't fret. Instead, focus upon God and upon His love for you. Then, ask Him for the wisdom to prioritize your life and the strength to fulfill your responsibilities. God will give you the energy to do the most important things on today's to-do list . . . if you ask Him. So ask Him.

Hope can give us life. It can provide energy that would otherwise do us in completely if we tried to operate in our own strength.

BARBARA JOHNSON

Living in a Fear-based World

*I sought the LORD, and he answered me; he delivered me
from all my fears.*

PSALM 34:4 NIV

We live in a fear-based world, a world where bad news travels at light speed and good news doesn't. These are troubled times, times when we have legitimate fears for the future of our nation, our world, and our families. But as Christians, we have every reason to live courageously. After all, the ultimate battle has already been fought and won on that faraway cross at Calvary.

Perhaps you, like countless other believers, have found your courage tested by the anxieties and fears that are an inevitable part of 21st-century life. If so, God wants to have a little chat with you. The next time you find your courage tested to the limit, God wants to remind you that He is not just near, He is here.

Your Heavenly Father is your Protector and your Deliverer. Call upon Him in your hour of need, and be comforted. Whatever your challenge, whatever your trouble, God can handle it. And will.

Fear knocked at the door. Faith answered. No one was there.

ANONYMOUS

Forgiveness Day by Day

See to it that no one repays evil for evil to anyone, but always pursue what is good for one another and for all.

1 Thessalonians 5:15 HCSB

If we could forgive other people "once and for all," life would be so much simpler, but it doesn't seem to work that way. Forgiveness is seldom a "one-time" decision; usually, forgiveness is a much more gradual process.

Each new day is a gift from God, but if your heart is filled with anger or regret, you simply won't be able to enjoy God's blessings. So, if you're struggling to forgive someone who has hurt you, do the right thing: spend a few quiet moments each morning thanking God for His gifts and asking Him to heal your broken heart. He can heal you—and He will heal you—if you don't grow tired of asking for His help.

Forgiveness is the key that unlocks the door of resentment and the handcuffs of hate. It is a power that breaks the chains of bitterness and the shackles of selfishness.

Corrie ten Boom

He Is Never Distant

*Do not be afraid or discouraged. For the LORD your God
is with you wherever you go.*

JOSHUA 1:9 NLT

God is not a distant being. He is not absent from our world; to the contrary, God's hand is actively involved in the smallest details of our lives. God is not "out there"; He is "right here," continuously reshaping His creation.

God is with you always, listening to your thoughts and prayers, watching over your every move. As the demands of everyday life weigh down upon you, you may be tempted to ignore God's presence or—worse yet—to rebel against His commandments. But, when you quiet yourself and acknowledge His presence, God touches your heart and restores your spirits.

At this very moment, God is seeking to work in you and through you. So why not let Him do it right now?

In heaven, we will see that nothing, absolutely nothing, was wasted, and that every tear counted and every cry was heard.

JONI EARECKSON TADA

Grace

But God, who is abundant in mercy, because of His great love that He had for us, made us alive with the Messiah even though we were dead in trespasses. By grace you are saved!

Ephesians 2:4-5 HCSB

Someone has said that GRACE stands for God's Redemption At Christ's Expense. It's true—God sent His Son so that we might be redeemed from our sins. In doing so, our Heavenly Father demonstrated His infinite mercy and His infinite love. We have received countless gifts from God, but none can compare with the gift of salvation. God's grace is the ultimate gift, and we owe Him the ultimate in thanksgiving.

The gift of eternal life is the priceless possession of everyone who accepts God's Son as Lord and Savior. We return our Savior's love by welcoming Him into our hearts and sharing His message and His love. When we do so, we are blessed today and forever.

There is no secret that can separate you from God's love; there is no secret that can separate you from His blessings; there is no secret that is worth keeping from His grace.

Serita Ann Jakes

His Surprising Plans

But as it is written in the Scriptures: "No one has ever seen this, and no one has ever heard about it. No one has ever imagined what God has prepared for those who love him."

1 CORINTHIANS 2:9 NCV

God has big plans for your life, wonderful, surprising plans . . . but He won't force those plans upon you. To the contrary, He has given you free will, the ability to make decisions on your own. Now, it's up to you to make those decisions wisely.

If you seek to live in accordance with God's plan for your life, you will study His Word, you will be attentive to His instructions, and you will be watchful for His signs. You will assiduously avoid those two terrible temptations: the temptation to sin and the temptation to squander time. And finally, you will listen carefully, even reverently, to the conscience that God has placed in your heart.

If you believe in a God who controls the big things, you have to believe in a God who controls the little things. It is we, of course, to whom things look "little" or "big."

ELISABETH ELLIOT

God's Armor

Finally, be strong in the Lord and in his mighty power. Put on the full armor of God so that you can take your stand against the devil's schemes.

EPHESIANS 6:10-11 NIV

In a world filled with dangers and temptations, God is the ultimate armor. In a world filled with misleading messages, God's Word is the ultimate truth. In a world filled with more frustrations than we can count, God's Son offers the ultimate peace. Will you accept God's peace and wear God's armor against the dangers of our world?

Sometimes, in the crush of everyday life, God may seem far away, but He is not. God is everywhere you have ever been and everywhere you will ever go. He is with you night and day; He knows your thoughts and your prayers. His is your ultimate Protector. And, when you earnestly seek His protection, you will find it because He is here—always—waiting patiently for you to reach out to Him.

Prayer is our pathway not only to divine protection, but also to a personal, intimate relationship with God.

SHIRLEY DOBSON

Hope Now

*Without wavering, let us hold tightly to the hope we say
we have, for God can be trusted to keep his promise.*

HEBREWS 10:23 NLT

Despite God's promises, despite Christ's love, and despite our countless blessings, we frail human beings can still lose hope from time to time. When we do, we need the encouragement of Christian friends, the life-changing power of prayer, and the healing truth of God's Holy Word.

If you find yourself falling into the spiritual traps of worry and discouragement, seek the healing touch of Jesus and the encouraging words of fellow Christians. And remember the words of our Savior: "These things I have spoken unto you, that in me ye might have peace. In the world ye shall have tribulation: but be of good cheer; I have overcome the world" (John 16:33 KJV). This world can be a place of trials and tribulations, but as believers, we are secure. God has promised us peace, joy, and eternal life. And, of course, God keeps His promises today, tomorrow, and forever.

Hope is the desire and the ability to move forward.

EMILIE BARNES

The Joy He Has Promised

Now I am coming to You, and I speak these things in the
world so that they may have My joy completed in them.

JOHN 17:13 HCSB

Christ intends that we should share His joy. Yet
sometimes, amid the inevitable hustle and
bustle of life-here-on-earth, we can forfeit—albeit
temporarily—the joy of Christ as we wrestle with the
challenges of daily living.

Corrie ten Boom correctly observed, "Jesus did not
promise to change the circumstances around us. He
promised great peace and pure joy to those who would
learn to believe that God actually controls all things."
So here's a prescription for better spiritual health: Learn
to trust God, and open the door of your soul to Christ.
When you do, He will most certainly give you the peace
and pure joy He has promised.

According to Jesus, it is God's will that His children be
filled with the joy of life.

CATHERINE MARSHALL

Unparalleled joy and victory come from allowing Christ
to do "the hard thing" with us.

BETH MOORE

And the Greatest of These

Love is patient, love is kind and is not jealous; love does not brag and is not arrogant, does not act unbecomingly; it does not seek its own, is not provoked, does not take into account a wrong suffered, does not rejoice in unrighteousness, but rejoices with the truth; bears all things, believes all things, hopes all things, endures all things.

1 Corinthians 13:4-7 NASB

The beautiful words of 1st Corinthians 13 remind us that love is God's commandment: "But now abide faith, hope, love, these three; but the greatest of these is love" (v. 13 NASB). Faith is important, of course. So, too, is hope. But, love is more important still. Christ showed His love for us on the cross, and, as Christians, we are called upon to return Christ's love by sharing it. Today, let us spread Christ's love to families, friends, and strangers by word and by deed.

God loves me as God loves all people, without qualification . . . . To be in the image of God means that all of us are made for the purpose of knowing and loving God and one another and of being loved in turn, not literally in the same way God knows and loves, but in a way appropriate to human beings.

Roberta Bondi

Passion and Purpose

May He grant you according to your heart's desire, and
fulfill all your purpose.

PSALM 20:4 NKJV

We all need to discover a purpose for our lives, a purpose that excites us and causes us to live each day with passion.

Anna Quindlen had this advice: "Consider the lilies of the field. Look at the fuzz on a baby's ear. Read in the backyard with the sun on your face. Learn to be happy. And think of life as a terminal illness, because, if you do, you will live it with joy and passion, as it ought to be lived."

If you have not yet discovered a passionate pursuit that blesses you and your world, don't allow yourself to become discouraged. Instead, keep searching and keep trusting that with God's help, you can—and will—find a meaningful way to serve your neighbors, your Creator, and yourself.

How much of our lives are, well, so daily. These very "daily" tasks could become a celebration of praise. "It is through consecration, " someone has said, "that drudgery is made divine."

GIGI GRAHAM TCHIVIDJIAN

Claim the Inner Peace

I leave you peace; my peace I give you. I do not give it to you as the world does. So don't let your hearts be troubled or afraid.

JOHN 14:27 NCV

Are you at peace with the direction of your life? Or are you still rushing after the illusion of "peace and happiness" that our world promises but cannot deliver? The answer to this simple question will determine, to a surprising extent, the direction and the quality of your day and your life.

Joyce Meyer observes, "We need to be at peace with our past, content with our present, and sure about our future, knowing they are all in God's hands."

Today, as a gift to yourself, to your family, and to your friends, claim the inner peace that is your spiritual birthright. It is offered freely; it is yours for the asking. So ask. And then share.

Peace does not mean to be in a place where there is no noise, trouble, or hard work. Peace means to be in the midst of all those things and still be calm in your heart.

CATHERINE MARSHALL

Your Primary Obligation

Everything that goes into a life of pleasing God has been miraculously given to us by getting to know, personally and intimately, the One who invited us to God. The best invitation we ever received!

2 PETER 1:3 MSG

When God created you, He equipped you with an assortment of talents and abilities that are uniquely yours. It's up to you to discover those talents and to use them, but the world may encourage you to do otherwise. At times, society will attempt to pigeonhole you, to standardize you, and to make you fit into a particular, preformed mold. Perhaps God has other plans.

Who will you try to please today: God or society? Your primary obligation is not to please imperfect men and women. Your obligation is to strive diligently to meet the expectations of an all-knowing and perfect God. Period.

If you are receiving your affirmation, love, self worth, joy, strength and acceptance from anywhere but God, He will shake it.

LISA BEVERE

Trusting His Answers

Trust in the LORD with all your heart; do not depend on your own understanding.

PROVERBS 3:5 NLT

God answers our prayers. What God does not do is this: He does not always answer our prayers as soon as we might like, and He does not always answer our prayers by saying "Yes." God isn't an order-taker, and He's not some sort of cosmic vending machine. Sometimes—even when we want something very badly—our loving Heavenly Father responds to our requests by saying "No," and we must accept His answer, even if we don't understand it.

God answers prayers not only according to our wishes but also according to His master plan. We cannot know that plan, but we can know the Planner . . . and we must trust His wisdom and His love. Always.

As I quietly abide in You and let Your life flow into me, what freedom it is to know that the Father does not see my threadbare patience or insufficient trust, rather only Your patience, Lord, and Your confidence that the Father has everything in hand. In Your faith I thank You right now for a more glorious answer to my prayer than I can imagine. Amen.

CATHERINE MARSHALL

Renewal and Celebration

And He who sits on the throne said, "Behold, I am making all things new."

REVELATION 21:5 NASB

Each new day offers countless opportunities to celebrate life and to serve God's children. But each day also offers countless opportunities to fall prey to the countless distractions of our difficult age.

Consider this day a new beginning. Consider it a fresh start, a renewed opportunity to serve your friends and family with willing hands and a loving heart.

Make your life a celebration. After all, your talents are unique, as are your opportunities. So the best time to really live—and really celebrate—is now.

Not every day of our lives is overflowing with joy and celebration. But there are moments when our hearts nearly burst within us for the sheer joy of being alive. The first sight of our newborn babies, the warmth of love in another's eyes, the fresh scent of rain on a hot summer's eve—moments like these renew in us a heartfelt appreciation for life.

GWEN ELLIS

Greatness According to God

A person should consider us in this way: as servants of Christ and managers of God's mysteries. In this regard, it is expected of managers that each one be found faithful.

1 CORINTHIANS 4:1-2 HCSB

How do you achieve greatness in the eyes of God? By making yourself a humble servant. Of course, being a fallible human being, you may feel the temptation to build yourself up in the eyes of your neighbors. Resist that temptation. Instead, serve your neighbors quietly and without fanfare. Find a need and fill it . . . humbly. Lend a helping hand and share a word of kindness . . . anonymously. Take the time to minister to those in need.

Then, when you have done your best to serve your neighbors and to serve your God, you can rest comfortably knowing that in the eyes of your Heavenly Father, you have achieved greatness. And God's eyes, after all, are the only ones that really count.

Through our service to others, God wants to influence our world for Him.

VONETTE BRIGHT

Tapped In to His Power

I can do everything through him that gives me strength.
PHILIPPIANS 4:13 NIV

Have you "tapped in" to the power of God? Have you turned your life and your heart over to Him, or are you muddling along under your own power? The answer to this question will determine the quality of your life here on earth and the destiny of your life throughout all eternity.

The Bible tells us that we can do all things through the power of our risen Savior, Jesus Christ. But what does the Bible say about our powers outside the will of Christ? The Bible teaches us that "the wages of sin is death" (Romans 6:23). Our challenge, then, is clear: we must place Christ where He belongs: at the very center of our lives. When we do so, we will surely discover that He offers us the strength to live victoriously in this world and eternally in the next.

When we reach the end of our strength, wisdom, and personal resources, we enter into the beginning of his glorious provisions.

PATSY CLAIRMONT

The Quality of Our Thoughts

May the words of my mouth and the thoughts of my heart
be pleasing to you, O LORD, my rock and my redeemer.

PSALM 19:14 NLT

Do you pay careful attention to the quality of your thoughts? And are you careful to direct those thoughts toward topics that are uplifting, enlightening, and pleasing to God? If so, congratulations. But if find that your thoughts are hijacked from time to time by the negativity that seems to have invaded our troubled world, you are not alone. Ours is a society that focuses on—and often glamorizes—the negative aspects of life, and that's unfortunate.

God intends that you experience joy and abundance. So, today and every day hereafter, celebrate the life that God has given you by focusing your thoughts upon those things that are worthy of praise (Philippians 4:8). And while you're at it, count your blessings instead of your hardships. When you do, you'll undoubtedly offer words of thanks to your Heavenly Father for gifts that are simply too numerous to count.

I am amazed at my own "rut-think" that periodically takes over.

MARILYN MEBERG

Acceptance Now

People may make plans in their minds, but the Lord decides what they will do.

PROVERBS 16:9 NCV

Sometimes, we must accept life on its terms, not our own. Life has a way of unfolding, not as we will, but as it will. And sometimes, there is precious little we can do to change things.

When events transpire that are beyond our control, we have a choice: we can either learn the art of acceptance, or we can make ourselves miserable as we struggle to change the unchangeable.

We must entrust the things we cannot change to God. Once we have done so, we can prayerfully and faithfully tackle the important work that He has placed before us: doing something about the things we can change . . . and doing it sooner rather than later.

Surrender to the Lord is not a tremendous sacrifice, not an agonizing performance. It is the most sensible thing you can do.

CORRIE TEN BOOM

Ask Him

Ask in my name, according to my will, and he'll most certainly give it to you. Your joy will be a river overflowing its banks!

JOHN 16:24 MSG

God gives the gifts; we, as believers, should accept them—but oftentimes, we don't. Why? Because we fail to trust our Heavenly Father completely, and because we are, at times, surprisingly stubborn. Luke 11 teaches us that God does not withhold spiritual gifts from those who ask. Our obligation, quite simply, is to ask for them.

Are you a woman who asks God to move mountains in your life, or are you expecting Him to stumble over molehills? Whatever the size of your challenges, God is big enough to handle them. Ask for His help today, with faith and with fervor, and then watch in amazement as your mountains begin to move.

God makes prayer as easy as possible for us. He's completely approachable and available, and He'll never mock or upbraid us for bringing our needs before Him.

SHIRLEY DOBSON

Faith or Fear?

Yea, though I walk through the valley of the shadow of death, I will fear no evil: for thou art with me; thy rod and thy staff they comfort me.

PSALM 23:4 KJV

Although God has guided us through our struggles and troubles many times before, it is easy for us to lose hope whenever we face adversity, uncertainty, or unwelcome changes.

The next time you find yourself facing a fear-provoking situation, remember that the One who calmed the wind and the waves is also your personal Savior. Then ask yourself which is stronger: your faith or your fear. The answer should be obvious. So, when the storm clouds form overhead and you find yourself being tossed on the stormy seas of life, remember this: Wherever you are, God is there, too. And, because He cares for you, you are protected.

Let nothing disturb you, nothing frighten you; all things are passing; God never changes.

ST. TERESA OF AVILA

Regular, Purposeful Worship

I was glad when they said to me, "Let us go to the house of the Lord."

PSALM 122:1 NLT

The Bible teaches that we should worship God in our hearts and in our churches (Acts 20:28). We have clear instructions to "feed the church of God" and to worship our Creator in the presence of fellow believers.

We live in a world that is teeming with temptations and distractions—a world where good and evil struggle in a constant battle to win our minds, our hearts, and our souls. Our challenge, of course, is to ensure that we cast our lot on the side of God. One way that we remain faithful to Him is through the practice of regular, purposeful worship with our families. When we worship the Father faithfully and fervently, we are blessed.

A living church gathers its members of all age groups and says, "Come! In this precious, unique, 'now' time, let's all go hard after God!"

ANNE ORTLUND

Making the Right Choices

The Lord says, "I will make you wise and show you where to go. I will guide you and watch over you."

PSALM 32:8 NCV

Are you facing a tough decision that has you totally confused? If so, here's a simple formula for making the right choice: let God decide. Instead of fretting about your future, pray about it.

When you consult your Heavenly Father early and often, you'll soon discover that God keeps His promises. He has promised to lead you, to protect you, and to guide you—and that's precisely what He will do. In time, God will quietly lead you along a path of His choosing, a path that is right for you.

So the next time you arrive at one of life's inevitable crossroads, consult God's roadmap (the Bible) and seek God's guidance (in prayer). When you do, you'll never stay lost for long.

The principle of making no decision without prayer keeps me from rushing in and committing myself before I consult God.

ELIZABETH GEORGE

Opportunities to Encourage

So encourage each other and give each other strength, just as you are doing now.

1 Thessalonians 5:11 NCV

Here's a question only you can answer: During a typical day, how many opportunities will you have to encourage other human beings? Unless you're living on a deserted island, the answer is "a lot!" And here's a follow-up question: How often do you take advantage of those opportunities? Hopefully, the answer is "more often than not."

Whether you realize it or not, you're surrounded by people who need an encouraging word, a helping hand, or a pat on the back. And every time you encourage one of these folks, you'll being doing God's will by obeying God's Word. So with no further ado, let the encouragement begin.

We can never untangle all the woes in other people's lives. We can't produce miracles overnight. But we can bring a cup of cool water to a thirsty soul, or a scoop of laughter to a lonely heart.

Barbara Johnson

Mountain-moving Faith

I assure you: If anyone says to this mountain, "Be lifted up and thrown into the sea," and does not doubt in his heart, but believes that what he says will happen, it will be done for him.

MARK 11:23 HCSB

Have you ever felt your faith in God slipping away? If so, you are not alone. Every life—including yours—is a series of successes and failures, celebrations and disappointments, joys and sorrows. But even when we feel very distant from God, God is never distant from us.

Jesus taught His disciples that if they had faith, they could move mountains. You can too. When you place your faith, your trust, indeed your life in the hands of Christ Jesus, you'll be amazed at the marvelous things He can do with you and through you. So strengthen your faith through praise, through worship, through Bible study, and through prayer. And trust God's plans. With Him, all things are possible, and He stands ready to open a world of possibilities to you if you have faith.

Faith is the quiet place within us where we don't get whiplash every time life tosses us a curve.

PATSY CLAIRMONT

Picking Up His Cross

*Summoning the crowd along with His disciples, He said
to them, "If anyone wants to be My follower, he must deny
himself, take up his cross, and follow Me."*

MARK 8:34 HCSB

When we have been saved by Christ, we can, if we
choose, become passive Christians. We can sit
back, secure in our own salvation, and let other believers
spread the healing message of Jesus. But to do so is
wrong. Instead, we are commanded to become disciples
of the One who has saved us, and to do otherwise is a
sin of omission with terrible consequences.

God's Word reminds us again and again that our
Savior intends that we pick up His cross and follow
Him. Are you willing to walk in the footsteps of the
One from Galilee? Jesus wants your attention and your
devotion. And He deserves both. And He deserves
them both now.

Jesus never asks us to give Him what we don't have. But
He does demand that we give Him all we do have if we
want to be a part of what He wishes to do in the lives of
those around us!

ANNE GRAHAM LOTZ

The Commandment to Be Generous

Freely you have received, freely give.

MATTHEW 10:8 NKJV

God's Word commands us to be generous, compassionate servants to those who need our support. As believers, we have been richly blessed by our Creator. We, in turn, are called to share our gifts, our possessions, our testimonies, and our talents.

Concentration camp survivor Corrie ten Boom correctly observed, "The measure of a life is not its duration but its donation." These words remind us that the quality of our lives is determined not by what we are able to take from others, but instead by what we are able to share with others.

The thread of generosity is woven into the very fabric of Christ's teachings. If we are to be disciples of Christ, we, too, must be cheerful, generous, courageous givers. Our Savior expects no less from us. And He deserves no less.

We can't do everything, but can we do anything more valuable than invest ourselves in another?

ELISABETH ELLIOT

A Righteous Life

*But seek first the kingdom of God and His righteousness,
and all these things shall be added to you.*

MATTHEW 6:33 NKJV

A righteous life has many components: faith, honesty, generosity, love, kindness, humility, gratitude, and worship, to name but a few. If we seek to follow the steps of our Savior, Jesus Christ, we must seek to live according to His commandments. In short, we must, to the best of our abilities, live according to the principles contained in God's Holy Word.

The Holy Bible contains thorough instructions which, if followed, lead to fulfillment, righteousness, and salvation. But, if we choose to ignore God's commandments, the results are as predictable as they are tragic. Let us follow God's commandments, and let us conduct our lives in such a way that we might be shining examples for those who have not yet found Christ.

A life lived in God is not lived on the plane of feelings, but of the will.

ELISABETH ELLIOT

Embraced by God

The unfailing love of the Lord never ends!

LAMENTATIONS 3:22 NLT

Every day of your life—indeed, every moment of your life—you are embraced by God. He is always with you, and His love for you is deeper and more profound than you can imagine. And now, precisely because you are a wondrous creation treasured by God, a question presents itself: What will you do in response to God's love? Will you ignore it or return it? Will you return it or neglect it? The decision, of course, is yours and yours alone.

When you open yourself to God's love, you feel differently about yourself, your neighbors, and your world. When you embrace God's love, you share His message and you obey His commandments.

When you accept the Father's grace and share the His love, you are blessed here on earth and throughout all eternity. Accept His love today.

We are so preciously loved by God that we cannot even comprehend it. No created being can ever know how much and how sweetly and tenderly God loves them.

JULIANA OF NORWICH

Following His Plan

The counsel of the LORD stands forever, the plans of His heart from generation to generation.

PSALM 33:11 NASB

You can expect a satisfying and fulfilling life when you follow God's plan for your life. But how can you discern God's will? You should begin by studying God's Word and obeying His commandments. You should watch carefully for His signs, and you should associate with fellow Christians who encourage your spiritual growth. And you should listen to that inner voice that speaks to you in the quiet moments of your daily devotionals.

God intends to use you in wonderful, unexpected ways if you let Him. The decision to seek God's plan and to follow it is yours and yours alone. The consequences of that decision have implications that are both profound and eternal, so choose carefully.

In the center of a hurricane there is absolute quiet and peace. There is no safer place than in the center of the will of God.

CORRIE TEN BOOM

Who Deserves the Credit?

But God, who comforts the humble, comforted us . . . .
2 CORINTHIANS 7:6 HCSB

When we experience success, it's easy to proclaim, "I did that!" But it's wrong. Dietrich Bonhoeffer was correct when he observed, "It is very easy to overestimate the importance of our own achievements in comparison with what we owe others." In other words, reality breeds humility.

Who are the greatest among us? Are they the proud and the powerful? Hardly. The greatest among us are the humble servants who care less for their own glory and more for God's glory. If we seek greatness in God's eyes, we must forever praise God's good works, not our own.

If you're tempted to overestimate your own accomplishments, resist that temptation. Instead of puffing out your chest and saying, "Look at me!", give credit where credit is due, starting with God. And, rest assured: There is no such thing as a self-made man. All of us are made by God, and He deserves the glory, not us.

We are never stronger than the moment we admit we are weak.

BETH MOORE

Laughter Keeps You Young

A merry heart makes a cheerful countenance . . . .
PROVERBS 15:13 NKJV

Would you like a proven formula for maintaining a youthful countenance? Here it is: Laugh as often as you can. It's a simple, yet effective, formula for a happier, healthier life.

Few sounds on earth can equal the happy reverberations of friends laughing together. Few joys in life can compare with a good laugh and a good friend to share it with. And it's also worth noting that God has given each of us the gift of laughter for a very good reason: to use it.

Hearty laughter is food for the soul and medicine for the heart. So do yourself this favor: acquire the habit of looking at the humorous side of life. When you do, you'll discover that, whatever your age, a good laugh can make you just a little bit younger.

Garden Tip: Learn to laugh at life: Life has a lighter side—look for it, especially when times are tough. Laughter is medicine for the soul, so take your medicine early and often. (Proverbs 17:22)

Expect a Miracle

Looking at them, Jesus said, "With men it is impossible, but not with God, because all things are possible with God."

MARK 10:27 HCSB

When you invite Christ to rule over your heart, you avail yourself of His power. And make no mistake about it: You and Christ, working together, can do miraculous things. In fact, miraculous things are exactly what Christ intends for you to do, but He won't force you to do great things on His behalf. The decision to become a full-fledged participant in His power is a decision that you must make for yourself.

Jesus made this promise: "I assure you: The one who believes in Me will also do the works that I do" (John 14:12 HCSB). In other words, when you put absolute faith in Christ, you can share in His power. So today, trust the Savior's promise—and expect a miracle in His name.

Our helplessness can be a healthy sign. This is always a good place to begin a task that seems completely impossible.

CATHERINE MARSHALL

A Marathon

Therefore since we also have such a large cloud of witnesses surrounding us, let us lay aside every weight and the sin that so easily ensnares us, and run with endurance the race that lies before us.

HEBREWS 12:1 HCSB

A well-lived life is like a marathon, not a sprint—it calls for preparation, determination, and lots of perseverance. As an example of perfect perseverance, we Christians need look no further than our Savior, Jesus Christ.

Jesus finished what He began. Despite His suffering, despite the shame of the cross, Jesus was steadfast in His faithfulness to God. We, too, must remain faithful, especially during times of hardship. Sometimes, God may answer our prayers with silence, and when He does, we must patiently persevere.

Remember this: whatever your problem, God can handle it. Your job is to keep persevering until He does.

God never gives up on you, so don't you ever give up on Him.

MARIE T. FREEMAN

Worship Every Day

Every day will I bless thee; and I will praise thy name for ever and ever.

PSALM 145:2 KJV

Too many of us, even well-intentioned believers, tend to "compartmentalize" our waking hours into a few familiar categories: work, rest, play, family time, and worship. As creatures of habit, we may find ourselves praising God only at particular times of the day or the week. But praise for our Creator should never be reserved for mealtimes, or bedtimes, or church. Instead, we should praise God all day, every day, to the greatest extent we can, with thanksgiving in our hearts, and with a song on our lips.

Today, find a little more time to lift your prayers to God, and thank Him for all that He has done. Every time you notice a gift from the Giver of all things good, praise Him. His works are marvelous, His gifts are beyond understanding, and His love endures forever.

Two wings are necessary to lift our souls toward God: prayer and praise. Prayer asks. Praise accepts the answer.

MRS. CHARLES E. COWMAN

Living on Purpose

It is God who works in you to will and to act according to his good purpose.

PHILIPPIANS 2:13 NIV

Life is best lived on purpose. And purpose, like everything else in the universe, begins with God. Whether you realize it or not, God has a plan for your life, a divine calling, a direction in which He is leading you. When you welcome God into your heart and establish a genuine relationship with Him, He will begin, in time, to make His purposes known.

Sometimes, God's intentions will be clear to you; other times, God's plan will seem uncertain at best. But even on those difficult days when you are unsure which way to turn, you must never lose sight of these overriding facts: God created you for a reason; He has important work for you to do; and He's waiting patiently for you to do it.

And the next step is up to you.

How we leave the world is more important than how we enter it.

JANETTE OKE

Seeking God

You will seek me and find me when you seek me with all your heart.

JEREMIAH 29:13 NIV

The words of Matthew 6 remind us that, as believers, we must seek God and His kingdom. And when we seek Him with our hearts open and our prayers lifted, we need not look far: God is with us always.

Sometimes, however, in the crush of our daily duties, God may seem far away, but He is not. God is everywhere we have ever been and everywhere we will ever go. He is with us night and day; He knows our thoughts and our prayers. And, when we earnestly seek Him, we will find Him because He is here, waiting patiently for us to reach out to Him.

Today, let us reach out to the Giver of all blessings. Let us turn to Him for guidance and for strength. Today, may we, who have been given so much, seek God and invite Him into every aspect of our lives. And, let us remember that no matter our circumstances, God never leaves us; He is here . . . always right here.

Speech and the Golden Rule

A good person produces good deeds and words season after season.

MATTHEW 12:35 MSG

The words of Matthew 7:12 are clear: "In everything, do to others what you would have them do to you, for this sums up the Law and the Prophets" (NIV). This commandment is, indeed, the Golden Rule for Christians of every generation. And if we are to observe the Golden Rule, we must be careful to speak words of encouragement, hope, and truth to all who cross our paths.

Sometimes, when we feel uplifted and secure, it is easy to speak kind words. Other times, when we are discouraged or tired, we can scarcely summon the energy to uplift ourselves, much less anyone else. But, God's commandment is clear: we must observe the Golden Rule "in everything."

A little kindly advice is better than a great deal of scolding.

FANNY CROSBY

A World Filled with Temptations

Look straight ahead, and fix your eyes on what lies before you. Mark out a straight path for your feet; then stick to the path and stay safe. Don't get sidetracked; keep your feet from following evil.

PROVERBS 4:25-27 NLT

Have you noticed that this world is filled to the brim with temptations? Unless you've been living the life of a hermit, you've observed that temptations, both great and small, are everywhere.

Some temptations are small; eating a second scoop of ice cream, for example, is tempting, but not very dangerous. Other temptations, however, are not nearly so harmless. The devil is working 24/7, and he's causing pain and heartache in more ways than ever before. Thankfully, in the battle against Satan, we are never alone. God is always with us, and He gives us the power to resist temptation whenever we ask Him for the strength to do so.

Temptation is not a sin. Even Jesus was tempted. The Lord Jesus gives you the strength needed to resist temptation.

CORRIE TEN BOOM

This Is the Day

This is the day the LORD has made; let us rejoice and be glad in it.

PSALM 118:24 NIV

The familiar words of Psalm 118:24 remind us of a profound yet simple truth: God created this day, and it's up to each of us to rejoice and to be grateful.

For Christian believers, every day begins and ends with God and His Son. Christ came to this earth to give us abundant life and eternal salvation. We give thanks to our Maker when we treasure each day and use it to the fullest.

So whatever this day holds for you, begin it and end it with God as your partner and Christ as your Savior. And throughout the day, give thanks to the One who created you and saved you. God's love for you is infinite. Accept it joyously and be thankful.

Submit each day to God, knowing that He is God over all your tomorrows.

KAY ARTHUR

Every day of our lives we make choices about how we're going to live that day.

LUCI SWINDOLL

We Belong to Him

Now return to the LORD your God, for He is gracious and compassionate, slow to anger, abounding in lovingkindness.

JOEL 2:13 NASB

When we sincerely call upon Him, God is a never-ending source of strength and courage. When we are weary, He gives us strength. When we see no hope, God reminds us of His promises. When we grieve, God wipes away our tears. Whatever our circumstances, God will protect us and care for us . . . if we let Him.

Are you in the midst of adversity or in the grips of temptation? If so, turn to God for strength. The Bible promises that you can do all things through the power of our risen Savior, Jesus Christ. Your challenge, then, is clear: you must place Christ where He belongs: at the very center of your life. When you do, you will discover that, yes, Jesus loves you and that, yes, He will give you direction and strength if you ask it in His name.

The unfolding of our friendship with the Father will be a never-ending revelation stretching on into eternity.

CATHERINE MARSHALL

No Shortcuts

Never be lazy in your work, but serve the Lord enthusiastically.

ROMANS 12:11 NLT

The world often tempts us with instant gratification: get rich—today; lose weight—today; have everything you want—today. Yet life's experiences and God's Word tell us that the best things in life require heaping helpings of both time and work.

It has been said, quite correctly, that there are no shortcuts to any place worth going. For believers, it's important to remember that hard work is not simply a proven way to get ahead, it's also part of God's plan for His children.

So do yourself this favor: don't look for shortcuts… because there aren't any.

You can't climb the ladder of life with your hands in your pockets.

BARBARA JOHNSON

I long to accomplish a great and noble task, but it is my chief duty to accomplish small tasks as if they were great and noble.

HELEN KELLER

Rebellion Against God

He who despises the word will be destroyed, But he who fears the commandment will be rewarded.

PROVERBS 13:13 NKJV

Since God created Adam and Eve, we human beings have been rebelling against our Creator. Why? Because we are unwilling to trust God's Word, and we are unwilling to follow His commandments. God has given us a guidebook for righteous living called the Holy Bible. It contains thorough instructions which, if followed, lead to fulfillment, righteousness and salvation. But, if we choose to ignore God's commandments, the results are as predictable as they are tragic.

Talking about God is easy; living by His commandments is considerably harder. But, unless we are willing to abide by God's laws, all of our righteous proclamations ring hollow. How can we best proclaim our love for the Lord? By obeying Him. And, for further instructions, read the manual.

There is sharp necessity for giving Christ absolute obedience. The devil bids for our complete self-will. To whatever extent we give this self-will the right to be master over our lives, we are, to an extent, giving Satan a toehold.

CATHERINE MARSHALL

His Answer to Our Guilt

If My people who are called by My name will humble themselves, and pray and seek My face, and turn from their wicked ways, then I will hear from heaven, and will forgive their sin and heal their land.

2 CHRONICLES 7:14 NKJV

All of us have sinned. Sometimes our sins result from our own stubborn rebellion against God's commandments. And sometimes, we are swept up in events that are beyond our abilities to control. Under either set of circumstances, we may experience intense feelings of guilt. But God has an answer for the guilt that we feel. That answer, of course, is His forgiveness. When we confess our wrongdoings and repent from them, we are forgiven by the One who created us.

Are you troubled by feelings of guilt or regret? If so, you must repent from your misdeeds, and you must ask your Heavenly Father for His forgiveness. When you do so, He will forgive you completely and without reservation. Then, you must forgive yourself just as God has forgiven you: thoroughly and unconditionally.

We have a decision to make—to turn away from sin or to be miserable and suffer the consequences of continual disobedience.

VONETTE BRIGHT

Trust the Shepherd

The Lord is my shepherd; I shall not want.

PSALM 23:1 KJV

In the 23rd Psalm, David teaches us that God is like a watchful shepherd caring for His flock. No wonder these verses have provided comfort and hope for generations of believers.

You are precious in the eyes of God. You are His priceless creation, made in His image, and protected by Him. God watches over every step you make and every breath you take, so you need never be afraid. But sometimes, fear has a way of slipping into the minds and hearts of even the most devout believers—and you are no exception.

On occasion, you will confront circumstances that trouble you to the very core of your soul. When you are afraid, trust in God. When you are worried, turn your concerns over to Him. When you are anxious, be still and listen for the quiet assurance of God's promises. And then, place your life in His hands. He is your Shepherd today and throughout eternity. Trust the Shepherd.

If a person fears God, he or she has no reason to fear anything else. On the other hand, if a person does not fear God, then fear becomes a way of life.

BETH MOORE

About Anger

When you are angry, do not sin, and be sure to stop being angry before the end of the day. Do not give the devil a way to defeat you.

EPHESIANS 4:26-27 NCV

Sometimes, anger is appropriate. Even Jesus became angry when confronted with the moneychangers in the temple. On occasion, you, like Jesus, will confront evil, and when you do, you may respond as He did: vigorously and without reservation. But, more often than not, your frustrations will be of the more mundane variety. As long as you live here on earth, you will face countless opportunities to lose your temper over small, relatively insignificant events: a traffic jam, a spilled cup of coffee, an inconsiderate comment, a broken promise. When you are tempted to lose your temper over the minor inconveniences of life, don't. Turn away from anger, hatred, bitterness, and regret. Turn instead to God.

Life is too short to spend it being angry, bored, or dull.

BARBARA JOHNSON

Anger unresolved will only bring you woe.

KAY ARTHUR

Beyond Bitterness

All bitterness, anger and wrath, insult and slander must be removed from you, along with all wickedness. And be kind and compassionate to one another, forgiving one another, just as God also forgave you in Christ.

EPHESIANS 4:31-32 HCSB

Are you mired in the quicksand of bitterness or regret? If so, you are not only disobeying God's Word, you are also wasting your time. The world holds few if any rewards for those who remain angrily focused upon the past. Still, the act of forgiveness is difficult for all but the most saintly men and women.

If there exists even one person—alive or dead—against whom you hold bitter feelings, it's time to forgive. Or, if you are embittered against yourself for some past mistake or shortcoming, it's finally time to forgive yourself and move on. Hatred, bitterness, and regret are not part of God's plan for your life. Forgiveness is.

Bitterness is a spiritual cancer, a rapidly growing malignancy that can consume your life. Bitterness cannot be ignored but must be healed at the very core, and only Christ can heal bitterness.

BETH MOORE

The Gift of Cheerfulness

A miserable heart means a miserable life; a cheerful heart fills the day with a song.

PROVERBS 15:15 MSG

Cheerfulness is a gift that we give to others and to ourselves. And, as believers who have been saved by a risen Christ, why shouldn't we be cheerful? The answer, of course, is that we have every reason to honor our Savior with joy in our hearts, smiles on our faces, and words of celebration on our lips.

Few things in life are more sad, or, for that matter, more absurd, than grumpy Christians. Christ promises us lives of abundance and joy if we accept His love and His grace. Yet sometimes, even the most righteous among us are beset by fits of ill temper and frustration. During these moments, we may not feel like turning our thoughts and prayers to Christ, but if we seek to gain perspective and peace, that's precisely what we must do.

When we bring sunshine into the lives of others, we're warmed by it ourselves. When we spill a little happiness, it splashes on us.

BARBARA JOHNSON

The New You

Therefore if anyone is in Christ, he is a new creature; the old things passed away; behold, new things have come.

2 CORINTHIANS 5:17 HCSB

Think, for a moment, about the "old" you, the person you were before you invited Christ to reign over your heart. Now, think about the "new" you, the person you have become since then. Is there a difference between the "old" you and the "new and improved" version? There should be! And that difference should be noticeable not only to you but also to others.

The Bible clearly teaches that when we welcome Christ into our hearts, we become new creations through Him. Our challenge, of course, is to behave ourselves like new creations. When we do, God fills our hearts, He blesses our endeavors, and He transforms our lives . . . forever.

For God is, indeed, a wonderful Father who longs to pour out His mercy upon us, and whose majesty is so great that He can transform us from deep within.

ST. TERESA OF AVILA

Beyond Your Hardships

He gives power to the weak, and to those who have no might He increases strength.

ISAIAH 40:29 NKJV

We Christians have many reasons to celebrate. God is in His heaven; Christ has risen, and we are the sheep of His flock. Yet sometimes, even the most devout Christian women can become discouraged. After all, we live in a world where expectations can be high and demands can be even higher. If you become discouraged with the direction of your day or your life, turn your thoughts and prayers to God. He is a God of possibility, not negativity. He will help you count your blessings instead of your hardships. And then, with a renewed spirit of optimism and hope, you can properly thank your Father in heaven for His blessings, for His love, and for His Son.

All discouragement is of the devil.

HANNAH WHITALL SMITH

When we yield to discouragement, it is usually because we give too much thought to the past or to the future.

ST. THÉRÈSE OF LISIEUX

Enthusiasm Now

Serve wholeheartedly, as if you were serving the Lord, not men.

EPHESIANS 6:7 NIV

D o you see each day as a glorious opportunity to serve God and to do His will? Are you enthused about life, or do you struggle through each day giving scarcely a thought to God's blessings? Are you constantly praising God for His gifts, and are you sharing His Good News with the world? And are you excited about the possibilities for service that God has placed before you, whether at home, at work, at church, or at school? You should be.

You are the recipient of Christ's sacrificial love. Accept it enthusiastically and share it fervently. Jesus deserves your enthusiasm; the world deserves it; and you deserve the experience of sharing it.

One of the great needs in the church today is for every Christian to become enthusiastic about his faith in Jesus Christ.

BILLY GRAHAM

The Wisdom to Respect Him

The fear of the Lord is the beginning of wisdom, and the knowledge of the Holy One is understanding.

PROVERBS 9:10 NKJV

Do you have a healthy, fearful respect for God's power? If so, you are both wise and obedient. And, because you are a thoughtful believer, you also understand that genuine wisdom begins with a profound appreciation for God's limitless power.

God praises humility and punishes pride. That's why God's greatest servants will always be those humble men and women who care less for their own glory and more for God's glory. In God's kingdom, the only way to achieve greatness is to shun it. And the only way to be wise is to understand these facts: God is great; He is all-knowing; and He is all-powerful. We must respect Him, and we must humbly obey His commandments, or we must accept the consequences of our misplaced pride.

God is God. Because He is God, He is worthy of my trust and obedience. I will find rest nowhere but in His holy will, a will that is unspeakably beyond my largest notions of what He is up to.

ELISABETH ELLIOT

God's Forgiveness

But God's mercy is great, and he loved us very much. Though we were spiritually dead because of the things we did against God, he gave us new life with Christ. You have been saved by God's grace.

EPHESIANS 2:4-5 NCV

God's power to forgive, like His love, is infinite. Despite your shortcomings, despite your sins, God offers you immediate forgiveness and eternal life when you accept Christ as your Savior.

When it comes to forgiveness, God doesn't play favorites and neither should you. You should forgive all those who have harmed you (not just the people who have asked for forgiveness or those who have made restitution). Complete forgiveness is God's way, and it should be your way, too. Anything less is an affront to Him and a burden to you.

God gives us permission to forget our past and the understanding to live our present. He said He will remember our sins no more. (Psalm 103:11-12)

SERITA ANN JAKES

Who Rules?

You shall have no other gods before Me.

EXODUS 20:3 NKJV

Who rules your heart? Is it God, or is it something else? Do you give God your firstfruits or your last? Have you given Christ your heart, your soul, your talents, your time, and your testimony, or have you given Him little more than a few hours each Sunday morning?

In the book of Exodus, God warns that we should place no gods before Him. Yet all too often, we place our Lord in second, third, or fourth place as we worship the gods of pride, greed, power, or lust. When we unwittingly place possessions or relationships above our love for the Creator, we must seek His forgiveness and repent from our sins.

Does God rule your heart? Make certain that the honest answer to this question is a resounding yes. In the life of every righteous believer, God comes first. And that's precisely the place that He deserves in your heart.

God is God whether we recognize it or not. Nothing about that can change, except us.

LISA WHELCHEL

His Love

You are my God, and I will give you thanks; you are my God, and I will exalt you. Give thanks to the LORD, for he is good; his love endures forever.

PSALM 118:28-29 NIV

God loves you—His love for you is deeper and more profound than you can imagine. God's love for you is so great that He sent His only Son to this earth to die for your sins and to offer you the priceless gift of eternal life.

You must decide whether or not to accept God's gift. Will you ignore it or embrace it? Will you return it or neglect it? Will you invite Christ to dwell in the center of your heart, or will you relegate Him to a position of lesser importance? The decision is yours, and so are the consequences. So choose wisely . . . and choose today.

To view ourselves through our Creator's loving, tear-filled eyes, we need to climb Calvary's hill and look down from the cross of Christ—for that is where God declared that we are worth the life of His precious Son.

SUSAN LENZKES

Infinite Possibilities

We know that all things work together for the good of those who love God: those who are called according to His purpose.

ROMANS 8:28 HCSB

Ours is a God of infinite possibilities. But sometimes, because of limited faith and limited understanding, we wrongly assume that God cannot or will not intervene in the affairs of mankind. Such assumptions are simply wrong.

Are you afraid to ask God to do big things in your life? Is your faith threadbare and worn? If so, it's time to abandon your doubts and reclaim your faith in God's promises.

God's Holy Word makes it clear: absolutely nothing is impossible for the Lord. And since the Bible means what it says, you can be comforted in the knowledge that the Creator of the universe can do miraculous things in your own life and in the lives of your loved ones. Your challenge, as a believer, is to take God at His word, and to expect the miraculous.

The task ahead of us is never as great as the Power behind us.

ANONYMOUS

His Love and Protection

The Lord your God in your midst, The Mighty One, will save; He will rejoice over you with gladness, He will quiet you with His love, He will rejoice over you with singing.

ZEPHANIAH 3:17 NKJV

The hand of God encircles us and comforts us in times of adversity. In times of hardship, He restores our strength; in times of sorrow, He dries our tears. When we are troubled, or weak, or embittered, God is as near as our next breath.

God has promised to protect us, and He intends to fulfill His promise. In a world filled with dangers and temptations, God is the ultimate armor. In a world filled with misleading messages, God's Word is the ultimate truth. In a world filled with more frustrations than we can count, God's Son offers the ultimate peace.

Will you accept God's peace and wear His armor against the dangers of our world? Hopefully so, because when you do, you can live courageously, knowing that you possess the ultimate protection: God's unfailing love for you.

He goes before us, follows behind us, and hems us safe inside the realm of His protection.

BETH MOORE

When Hope Slips Away

Hope deferred makes the heart sick.

PROVERBS 13:12 NKJV

Have you ever felt hope for the future slipping away? If so, you have temporarily lost sight of the hope that we, as believers, must place in the promises of our Heavenly Father. If you are feeling discouraged, worried, or worse, remember the words of Psalm 31: "Be of good courage, and He shall strengthen your heart."

Because we are saved by a risen Christ, we can have hope for the future, no matter how desperate our circumstances may seem. After all, God has promised that we are His throughout eternity. And, He has told us that we must place our hopes in Him.

Of course, we will face disappointments and failures, but these are only temporary defeats. Of course, this world can be a place of trials and tribulations, but we are secure. God has promised us peace, joy, and eternal life. And God keeps His promises today, tomorrow, and forever.

God's Word never said we were not to grieve our losses. It says we are not to grieve as those who have no hope (1 Thessalonians 4:13). Big Difference.

BETH MOORE

Share His Joy

The Lord reigns; let the earth rejoice.

PSALM 97:1 NKJV

The Lord intends that believers should share His love with His joy in their hearts. Yet sometimes, amid the inevitable hustle and bustle of life-here-on-earth, we can forfeit—albeit temporarily—God's joy as we wrestle with the challenges of daily living.

Joni Eareckson Tada spoke for Christian women of every generation when she observed, "I wanted the deepest part of me to vibrate with that ancient yet familiar longing, that desire for something that would fill and overflow my soul."

If, today, your heart is heavy, open the door of your soul to Christ. He will give you peace and joy. And if you already have the joy of Christ in your heart, share it freely, just as Christ freely shared His joy with you.

Claim the joy that is yours. Pray. And know that your joy is used by God to reach others.

KAY ARTHUR

Every morning is a fresh opportunity to find God's extraordinary joy in the most ordinary places.

JANET. L. WEAVER

Loving God

*Love the L*ORD *your God with all your heart and with all
your soul and with all your strength.*

DEUTERONOMY 6:5 NIV

If you want to know God in a more meaningful way,
you'll need to open up your heart and let Him in.

C. S. Lewis observed, "A person's spiritual health is
exactly proportional to his love for God." If you hope to
receive a full measure of God's spiritual blessings, you
must invite your Creator to rule over your heart. When
you honor God in this way, His love expands to fill your
heart and bless your life.

St. Augustine wrote, "I love you, Lord, not
doubtingly, but with absolute certainty. Your Word beat
upon my heart until I fell in love with you, and now the
universe and everything in it tells me to love you."

Today, open your heart to the Father. And let your
obedience be a fitting response to His never-ending
love.

If you love God enough to ask Him what you can do for
Him, then your relationship is growing deep.

STORMIE OMARTIAN

Making Peace with the Past

Do not remember the past events, pay no attention to things of old. Look, I am about to do something new; even now it is coming. Do you not see it? Indeed, I will make a way in the wilderness, rivers in the desert.

ISAIAH 43:18-19 HCSB

Have you made peace with your past? If so, congratulations. But, if you are mired in the quicksand of regret, it's time to plan your escape. How can you do so? By accepting what has been and by trusting God for what will be.

Because you are human, you may be slow to forget yesterday's disappointments; if so you are not alone. But if you sincerely seek to focus your hopes and energies on the future, then you must find ways to accept the past, no matter how difficult it may be to do so.

If you have not yet made peace with the past, today is the day to declare an end to all hostilities. When you do, you can then turn your thoughts to wondrous promises of God and to the glorious future that He has in store for you.

We can't just put our pasts behind us. We've got to put our pasts in front of God.

BETH MOORE

His Peace

But now in Christ Jesus you who once were far off have been brought near by the blood of Christ. For He Himself is our peace.

EPHESIANS 2:13-14 NKJV

On many occasions, our outer struggles are simply manifestations of the inner conflicts that we feel when we stray from God's path. What's needed is a refresher course in God's promise of peace. The beautiful words of John 14:27 remind us that Jesus offers peace, not as the world gives, but as He alone gives: "Peace I leave with you. My peace I give to you. I do not give to you as the world gives. Your heart must not be troubled or fearful" (HCSB).

As believers, our challenge is straightforward: we should welcome Christ's peace into our hearts and then, as best we can, share His peace with our neighbors.

Today, as a gift to yourself, to your family, and to your friends, invite Christ to preside over every aspect of your life. It's the best way to live and the surest path to peace . . . today and forever.

Our soul can never have rest in things that are beneath itself.

JULIANA OF NORWICH

Keeping Possessions in Perspective

Then Jesus said to them, "Be careful and guard against all kinds of greed. Life is not measured by how much one owns."

Luke 12:15 NCV

Earthly riches are temporary: here today and soon gone forever. Spiritual riches, on the other hand, are permanent: ours today, ours tomorrow, ours throughout eternity. Yet all too often, we focus our thoughts and energies on the accumulation of earthly treasures, leaving precious little time to accumulate the only treasures that really matter: the spiritual kind.

Our material possessions have the potential to do great good or terrible harm, depending upon how we choose to use them. As believers, our instructions are clear: we must use our possessions in accordance with God's commandments, and we must be faithful stewards of the gifts He has seen fit to bestow upon us.

Today, let us honor God by placing no other gods before Him. God comes first; everything else comes next—and "everything else" most certainly includes all of our earthly possessions.

Why is love of gold more potent than love of souls?

Lottie Moon

Pride in Times of Abundance

When pride comes, disgrace follows, but with humility comes wisdom.

PROVERBS 11:2 HCSB

Sometimes, we are tested more in times of plenty than we are in times of privation. When we experience life's difficult days, we may be more likely to turn our thoughts and hearts to God. But in times of plenty, when the sun is shining and our minds are at ease, we may be tempted to believe that our good fortune is entirely of our own making. Nothing could be further from the truth. God plays a hand in every aspect of everyday life, and for the blessings that we receive, we must offer thanks and praise to Him, not to ourselves.

Have you been blessed by God? Are you enjoying the abundance He has promised? If so, praise Him for His gifts. Praise Him faithfully and humbly. And don't, for a single moment, allow a prideful heart to separate you from the blessings of your loving Father.

It was as important to me that my children be no more self-righteous than they were unrighteous. In His Gospels, Christ seemed far more tolerant of a repentant sinner than a self-righteous, self-proclaimed saint.

BETH MOORE

He Renews

Finally, be strengthened by the Lord and by His vast strength.

EPHESIANS 6:10 HCSB

God's Word is clear: When we genuinely lift our hearts and prayers to Him, He renews our strength. Are you almost too weary to lift your head? Then bow it. Offer your concerns and your fears to your Father in heaven. He is always at your side, offering His love and His strength.

Are you troubled or anxious? Take your anxieties to God in prayer. Are you weak or worried? Delve deeply into God's Holy Word and sense His presence in the quiet moments of the early morning. Are you spiritually exhausted? Call upon fellow believers to support you, and call upon Christ to renew your spirit and your life. Your Savior will not let you down. To the contrary, He will lift you up when you ask Him to do so. So what, dear friend, are you waiting for?

Be still, and in the quiet moments, listen to the voice of your Heavenly Father. His words can renew your spirit—no one knows you and your needs like He does.

JANET L. WEAVER SMITH

Opportunities for Service

So let us try to do what makes peace and helps one another.

ROMANS 14:19 NCV

You're a special person, created by God, and He has unique work for you to do. Do you acknowledge your own uniqueness, and do you celebrate the one-of-kind opportunities that God has placed before you? Hopefully so. But if you're like too many women, you may have fallen into a trap—the trap of taking yourself and your opportunities for granted.

God created you with a surprising array of talents, and He placed you precisely where you are—at a time and place of His choosing. God has done His part by giving you life, love, blessings, and more opportunities than you can count. Your particular situation is unique and so are your opportunities for service.

And the rest is up to you.

God has lots of folks who intend to go to work for him "some day." What He needs is more people who are willing to work for Him today.

MARIE T. FREEMAN

Rebels Beware

Whoever is stubborn after being corrected many times will suddenly be hurt beyond cure.

PROVERBS 29:1 NCV

Since the days of Adam and Eve, human beings have been strong-willed and rebellious. Our rebellion stems, in large part, from an intense desire to do things "our way" instead of "God's way." But when we pridefully choose to forsake God's path for our lives, we do ourselves a sincere injustice . . . and we are penalized because of our stubbornness.

God's Word warns us to be humble, not prideful. God instructs us to be obedient, not rebellious. God wants us to do things His way. When we do, we reap a bountiful harvest of blessings—more blessings than we can count. But when we pridefully rebel against our Creator, we sow the seeds of our own destruction, and we reap a sad, sparse, bitter harvest. May we sow—and reap—accordingly.

Christians see sin for what it is: willful rebellion against the rulership of God in their lives. And in turning from their sin, they have embraced God's only means of dealing with sin: Jesus.

KAY ARTHUR

Directing Your Thoughts

And now, dear brothers and sisters, let me say one more thing as I close this letter. Fix your thoughts on what is true and honorable and right. Think about things that are pure and lovely and admirable. Think about things that are excellent and worthy of praise.

PHILIPPIANS 4:8 NLT

How will you direct your thoughts today? Will you obey the words of Philippians 4:8 by dwelling upon those things that are honorable, true, and worthy of praise? Or will you allow your thoughts to be hijacked by the negativity that seems to dominate our troubled world?

Are you fearful, angry, bored, or worried? Are you so preoccupied with the concerns of this day that you fail to thank God for the promise of eternity? Are you confused, bitter, or pessimistic? If so, God wants to have a little talk with you. He wants to remind you of His infinite love and His boundless grace. As you contemplate these things, and as you give thanks for God's blessings, negativity should no longer dominate your day or your life.

Accepting Christ

We know very well that we are not set right with God by rule-keeping but only through personal faith in Jesus Christ.

GALATIANS 2:16 MSG

God's love for you is deeper and more profound than you can imagine. God's love for you is so great that He sent His only Son to this earth to die for your sins and to offer you the priceless gift of eternal life. Now, you must decide whether or not to accept God's gift. Will you ignore it or embrace it? Will you return it or neglect it? Will you accept Christ, or will you turn from Him?

Your decision to accept Christ is the pivotal decision of your life. It is a decision that you cannot ignore. It is a decision that is yours and yours alone. It is a decision with profound consequences, both earthly and eternal. Accept God's gift: Accept Christ today.

Every person who has ever been born has the sovereign right to make this same choice—to receive Jesus Christ by faith as God's revelation of Himself, or to reject Him.

ANNE GRAHAM LOTZ

What's Your Attitude?

Set your minds on what is above, not on what is on the earth.

COLOSSIANS 3:2 HCSB

What's your attitude today? Are you fearful, angry, bored, or worried? Are you worried more about pleasing your friends than about pleasing your God? Are you confused, bitter or pessimistic? If so, God wants to have a little talk with you.

God created you in His own image, and He wants you to experience joy and abundance. But, God will not force His joy upon you; you must claim it for yourself. So today, and every day thereafter, celebrate this life that God has given you. Think optimistically about yourself and your future. Give thanks to the One who has given you everything, and trust in your heart that He wants to give you so much more.

I became aware of one very important concept I had missed before: my attitude—not my circumstances— was what was making me unhappy.

VONETTE BRIGHT

Giving Thanks to the Giver

Is anyone happy? Let him sing songs of praise.

JAMES 5:13 NIV

Psalm 100 reminds us that the entire earth should "Shout for joy to the Lord." As God's children, we are blessed beyond measure, but sometimes, as busy women living in a demanding world, we are slow to count our gifts and even slower to give thanks to the Giver.

Our blessings include life and health, family and friends, freedom and possessions—for starters. And, the gifts we receive from God are multiplied when we share them. May we always give thanks to God for His blessings, and may we always demonstrate our gratitude by sharing our gifts with others.

The 118th Psalm reminds us that, "This is the day which the LORD has made; let us rejoice and be glad in it" (v. 24 NASB). May we celebrate this day and the One who created it.

I am to praise God for all things, regardless of where they seem to originate. Doing this is the key to receiving the blessings of God. Praise will wash away my resentments.

CATHERINE MARSHALL

Involved in His Church

The church, you see, is not peripheral to the world; the world is peripheral to the church. The church is Christ's body, in which he speaks and acts, by which he fills everything with his presence.

EPHESIANS 1:23 MSG

One way that we come to know God is by involving ourselves in His church.

In the Book of Acts, Luke reminds us to "feed the church of God" (20:28). As Christians who have been saved by a loving, compassionate Creator, we are compelled not only to worship Him in our hearts but also to worship Him in the presence of fellow believers.

Do you attend church regularly? And when you attend, are you an active participant, or are you just taking up space? The answer to these questions will have a profound impact on the quality and direction of your spiritual journey.

So do yourself a favor: become actively involved in your church. Don't just go to church out of habit. Go to church out of a sincere desire to know and worship God. When you do, you'll be blessed by the One who sent His Son to die so that you might have everlasting life.

When Solutions Aren't Easy

For God has not given us a spirit of fearfulness, but one of power, love, and sound judgment.

2 TIMOTHY 1:7 HCSB

Sometimes, we all face problems that defy easy solutions. If you find yourself facing a difficult decision, here's a simple formula for making the right choice: let God decide. Instead of fretting about your future, pray about it.

When you consult your Heavenly Father early and often, you'll soon discover that the quiet moments you spend with God can be very helpful. Many times, God will quietly lead you along a path of His choosing, a path that is right for you.

So the next time you arrive at one of life's inevitable crossroads, take a moment or two to bow your head and have a chat with the Ultimate Advisor. When you do, you'll never stay lost for long.

The Reference Point for the Christian is the Bible. All values, judgments, and attitudes must be gauged in relationship to this Reference Point.

RUTH BELL GRAHAM

Guarding Against Evil

Turn from your evil ways and keep My commandments and statutes according to all the law I commanded your ancestors and sent to you through My servants the prophets.

2 Kings 17:13 HCSB

This world contains countless opportunities to stray from God's will. Temptations are everywhere, and the devil, it seems, never takes a day off. Our task, as believers, is to turn away from temptation and to place our lives squarely in the center of God's will.

In his letter to Jewish Christians, Peter offered a stern warning: "Your adversary, the devil, prowls around like a roaring lion, seeking someone to devour" (1 Peter 5:8 NASB). What was true in New Testament times is equally true in our own. Evil is indeed abroad in the world, and Satan continues to sow the seeds of destruction far and wide. As Christians, we must guard our hearts by earnestly wrapping ourselves in the protection of God's Holy Word. When we do, we are protected.

Light is stronger than darkness—darkness cannot "comprehend" or "overcome" it.

ANNE GRAHAM LOTZ

Faith for the Future

For we walk by faith, not by sight.

2 CORINTHIANS 5:7 NKJV

The first element of a successful life is faith: faith in God, faith in His Son, and faith in His promises. If we place our lives in God's hands, our faith is rewarded in ways that we—as human beings with clouded vision and limited understanding—can scarcely comprehend. But, if we seek to rely solely upon our own resources, or if we seek earthly success outside the boundaries of God's commandments, we reap a bitter harvest for ourselves and for our loved ones.

Do you desire the abundance and success that God has promised? Then trust Him today and every day that you live. Trust Him with every aspect of your life. Trust His promises, and trust in the saving grace of His only begotten Son. Then, when you have entrusted your future to the Giver of all things good, rest assured that your future is secure, not only for today, but also for all eternity.

Faith keeps the person who keeps the faith.

MOTHER TERESA

Giving Thanks to the Creator

In everything give thanks; for this is the will of God in Christ Jesus for you.

1 THESSALONIANS 5:18 NKJV

If you sat down and began counting your blessings, how long would it take? A very, very long time! Your blessings include life, freedom, family, friends, talents, and possessions, for starters. But, your greatest blessing—a gift that is yours for the asking—is God's gift of salvation through Christ Jesus.

Today, give thanks for your blessings by accepting them fully (with open arms) and by sharing them generously (with a thankful heart).

Billy Graham had this advice: "Think of the blessings we so easily take for granted: Life itself; preservation from danger; every bit of health we enjoy; every hour of liberty; the ability to see, to hear, to speak, to think, and to imagine all this comes from the hand of God." And that's sound advice for Christians—like you—who have been blessed beyond measure.

God is in control, and therefore in everything I can give thanks, not because of the situation, but because of the One who directs and rules over it.

KAY ARTHUR

Freely Give

If you give, you will receive. Your gift will return to you in full measure, pressed down, shaken together to make room for more, and running over. Whatever measure you use in giving—large or small—it will be used to measure what is given back to you.

LUKE 6:38 NLT

The words are familiar to those who study God's Word: "Freely you have received, freely give" (Matthew 10:8 NKJV). As followers of Christ, we have been given so much by God. In return, we must give freely of our time, our possessions, our testimonies, and our love.

Your salvation was earned at a terrible price: Christ gave His life for you on the cross at Calvary. Christ's gift is priceless, yet when you accept Jesus as your personal Savior, His gift of eternal life costs you nothing. From those to whom much has been given, much is required. And because you have received the gift of salvation, you are now called by God to be a cheerful, generous steward of the gifts He has placed under your care.

Today and every day, let Christ's words be your guide and let His eternal love fill your heart. When you do, your stewardship will be a reflection of your love for Him, and that's exactly as it should be. After all, He loved you first.

God's Correction

My child, do not reject the Lord's discipline, and don't get angry when he corrects you.

PROVERBS 3:11 NCV

The hand of God corrects us when we disobey His commandments. The hand of God guides us when we stray from His chosen path. When our behavior is inconsistent with God's will, our Heavenly Father inevitably disciplines us in the same fashion that a loving parent disciplines a wayward child.

Hebrews 12:5 reminds us that when God chastises us, we should accept His discipline without bitterness or despair. We should, instead, look upon God's instruction as an occasion to repent from our sins, to reorder our priorities, and to realign our lives.

God's correction is purposeful: He intends to guide us back to Him. When we trust God completely and without reservation, He gives us the strength to meet any challenge, the courage to face any trial, and the wisdom to live in His righteousness and in His peace.

God is a God of unconditional, unremitting love, a love that corrects and chastens but never ceases.

KAY ARTHUR

God's Love, God's Power

The Lord your God in your midst, The Mighty One, will save; He will rejoice over you with gladness, He will quiet you with His love, He will rejoice over you with singing.

ZEPHANIAH 3:17 NKJV

God's power is not burdened by boundaries or by limitations—and neither, for that matter, is His love. The love that flows from the heart of God is infinite—and today offers yet another opportunity to celebrate that love.

Have you made God the cornerstone of your life, or is He relegated to a few hours on Sunday morning? Have you genuinely allowed God to reign over every corner of your heart, or have you attempted to place Him in a spiritual compartment? The answer to these questions will determine the direction of your day and the direction of your life.

God's love for you is deeper and more profound than you can fathom. In times of trouble, He will comfort you; in times of sorrow, He will dry your tears. When you are or weak or sorrowful, God is as near as your next breath. He stands at the door of your heart and waits. Welcome Him in and allow Him to rule. And then, accept the peace, and the power, and the protection, and the abundance that only God can give.

His Golden Rule

*If you really carry out the royal law prescribed in Scripture,
You shall love your neighbor as yourself, you are doing
well.*

JAMES 2:8 HCSB

As Christians, we are instructed to be courteous and compassionate. As believers, we are called to be gracious, humble, gentle, and kind. But sometimes, we fall short. Sometimes, amid the busyness and confusion of everyday life, we may neglect to share a kind word or a kind deed. This oversight hurts others, and it hurts us as well.

Today, slow yourself down and be alert for those who need your smile, your kind words, or your helping hand. Make kindness a centerpiece of your dealings with others. They will be blessed, and you will be, too. So make this promise to yourself and keep it: honor Christ by obeying His Golden Rule. He deserves no less. And neither, for that matter, do they.

It is one of the most beautiful compensations of life that no one can sincerely try to help another without helping herself.

BARBARA JOHNSON

Imitating Christ

For I have given you an example that you also should do just as I have done for you.

JOHN 13:15 HCSB

Life is a series of decisions and choices. Each day, we make countless decisions that can bring us closer to God . . . or not. When we live according to God's commandments, we reap bountiful rewards: abundance, hope, and peace, for starters. But, when we turn our backs upon God by disobeying Him, we bring needless suffering upon ourselves and our families.

Do you seek to walk in the footsteps of the One from Galilee, or will you choose another path? If you sincerely seek God's peace and His blessings, then you must strive to imitate God's Son.

Thomas Brooks spoke for believers of every generation when he observed, "Christ is the sun, and all the watches of our lives should be set by the dial of his motion." Christ, indeed, is the ultimate Savior of mankind and the personal Savior of those who believe in Him. As His servants, we should walk in His footsteps as we share His love and His message with a world that needs both.

The Glorious Gift of Life

Seek the Lord, and ye shall live . . . .

AMOS 5:6 KJV

Life is a glorious gift from God. Treat it that way. This day, like every other, is filled to the brim with opportunities, challenges, and choices. But, no choice that you make is more important than the choice you make concerning God. Today, you will either place Him at the center of your life—or not—and the consequences of that choice have implications that are both temporal and eternal.

Sometimes, we don't intentionally neglect God; we simply allow ourselves to become overwhelmed with the demands of everyday life. And then, without our even realizing it, we gradually drift away from the One we need most. Thankfully, God never drifts away from us. He remains always present, always steadfast, always loving.

As you begin this day, place God and His Son where they belong: in your head, in your prayers, on your lips, and in your heart. And then, with God as your guide and companion, let the journey begin . . .

Life is not a journey you want to make on autopilot.

PAULA RINEHART

On Mistakes and Opportunities

I used to wander off until you disciplined me; but now I closely follow your word.

PSALM 119:67 NLT

Have you experienced a recent setback? If so, look for the lesson that God is trying to teach you. Instead of complaining about life's sad state of affairs, learn what needs to be learned, change what needs to be changed, and move on. View failure as an opportunity to reassess God's will for your life. And while you're at it, consider life's inevitable disappointments to be powerful opportunities to learn more—more about yourself, more about your circumstances, and more about your world.

Life can be difficult at times. And everybody (including you) makes mistakes. Your job is to make them only once. And how can you do that? By learning the lessons of tough times sooner rather than later, that's how.

Mistakes offer the possibility for redemption and a new start in God's kingdom. No matter what you're guilty of, God can restore your innocence.

BARBARA JOHNSON

The Need to Persevere

Patient endurance is what you need now, so you will continue to do God's will. Then you will receive all that he has promised.

HEBREWS 10:36 NLT

If you've led a perfect life with absolutely no foul ups, blunders, mistakes, or flops, you can skip this chapter. But if you're like the rest of us, you know that occasional disappointments and failures are an inevitable part of life. These setbacks are simply the price of growing up and learning about life. But even when you experience bitter disappointments, you must never lose faith.

When times are tough, the Bible teaches us to persevere: "For you need endurance, so that after you have done God's will, you may receive what was promised." These reassuring words from Hebrews 10:36 (HCSB) remind us that when we persevere, we will eventually receive that which God has promised. Even when we fail, God is faithful. What's required of us is perseverance, not perfection.

When we encounter the inevitable difficulties of life-here-on-earth, God stands ready to protect us. And, while we are waiting for God's plans to unfold, we can be comforted in the knowledge that our Creator can overcome any obstacle, even if we cannot.

The Best Time to Praise Him

But as for me, I will always have hope; I will praise you more and more.

Psalm 71:14 NIV

When is the best time to praise God? In church? Before dinner is served? When we tuck little children into bed? None of the above. The best time to praise God is all day, every day, to the greatest extent we can, with thanksgiving in our hearts.

Too many of us, even well-intentioned believers, tend to "compartmentalize" our waking hours into a few familiar categories: work, rest, play, family time, and worship. To do so is a mistake. Worship and praise should be woven into the fabric of everything we do; it should never be relegated to a weekly three-hour visit to church on Sunday morning.

Mrs. Charles E. Cowman, the author of the classic devotional text *Streams in the Desert*, wrote, "Two wings are necessary to lift our souls toward God: prayer and praise. Prayer asks. Praise accepts the answer." Today, find a little more time to lift your concerns to God in prayer, and praise Him for all that He has done. He's listening . . . and He wants to hear from you.

He Protects

Our help is in the name of the Lord, the Maker of heaven and earth.

PSALM 124:8 HCSB

Once you finally discover God's purpose for your life, your search will be over and your life will be complete…right? Wrong! Your search to discover God's plan for your life not a destination to be reached; it is a path to be traveled, a journey that unfolds day by day. And, that's exactly how often you should seek direction from your Creator: one day at a time, each day followed by the next, without exception.

Life is a series of changes followed by a series of adjustments: how far you go depends upon how well you adjust. Sometimes, the adjustments are easy; sometimes, they are not. But you can be comforted in the knowledge that your Heavenly Father is the rock that cannot be shaken. His Word promises, "I am the Lord, I do not change" (Malachi 3:6 NKJV).

Have you endured changes that left your head spinning and your heart aching? If so, seek protection from the One who cannot be moved. The same God who created the universe will protect you if you ask Him…so ask Him…and then serve Him with willing hands and a trusting heart.

Conduct That Is Worthy of Him

By this we know that we have come to know Him, if we keep His commandments.

1 JOHN 2:3 NASB

How do others know that we are followers of Christ? By our words and by our actions. And when it comes to proclaiming our faith, the actions we take are far more important than the proclamations we make.

Is your conduct a worthy example for believers and non-believers alike? Is your behavior a testimony to the spiritual abundance that is available to those who allow Christ to reign over their hearts? If so, you are wise: congratulations. But if you're like most of us, then you know that some important aspect of your life could stand improvement. If so, today is the perfect day to make yourself a living, breathing example of the wonderful changes that Christ can make in the lives of those who choose to walk with Him.

Either God's Word keeps you from sin, or sin keeps you from God's Word.

CORRIE TEN BOOM

Wise Words

*From a wise mind comes wise speech; the words of the wise
are persuasive.*

PROVERBS 16:23 NLT

Think . . . pause . . . then speak: How wise is the woman who can communicate in this way. But all too often, in the rush to have ourselves heard, we speak first and think next . . . with unfortunate results.

God's Word reminds us that "Reckless words pierce like a sword, but the tongue of the wise brings healing" (Proverbs 12:18 NIV). If we seek to be a source of encouragement to friends and family, then we must measure our words carefully. Words are important: they can hurt or heal. Words can uplift us or discourage us, and reckless words, spoken in haste, cannot be erased.

Today, seek to encourage all who cross your path. Measure your words carefully. Speak wisely, not impulsively. Use words of kindness and praise, not words of anger or derision. Remember that you have the power to heal others or to injure them, to lift others up or to hold them back. When you lift them up, your wisdom will bring healing and comfort to a world that needs both.

The battle of the tongue is won not in the mouth, but in the heart.

ANNIE CHAPMAN

Sharing Your Testimony

And I say to you, anyone who acknowledges Me before men, the Son of Man will also acknowledge him before the angels of God.

LUKE 12:8 HCSB

In his second letter to Timothy, Paul offers a message to believers of every generation when he writes, "God has not given us a spirit of timidity" (1:7 NASB). Paul's meaning is crystal clear: When sharing our testimonies, we, as Christians, must be courageous, forthright, and unashamed.

We live in a world that desperately needs the healing message of Christ Jesus. Every believer, each in his or her own way, bears a personal responsibility for sharing that message. If you are a believer in Christ, you know how He has touched your heart and changed your life. Now it's your turn to share the Good News with others. And remember: today is the perfect time to share your testimony because tomorrow may quite simply be too late.

Those who are not yet in the family of Christ need us to be his hands, his feet, his eyes, his ears, and his voice to help them find God's love.

DORIS GREIG

He Changes You

I'm baptizing you here in the river, turning your old life in for a kingdom life. His baptism—a holy baptism by the Holy Spirit—will change you from the inside out.

MARK 1:8 MSG

God has the power to transform your life if you invite Him to do so. Your decision is straightforward: whether or not to allow the Father's transforming power to work in you and through you. God stands at the door and waits; all you must do is knock. When you do, God always answers.

Sometimes, the demands of daily life may drain you of strength or rob you of the joy that is rightfully yours in Christ. But even on your darkest day, you may be comforted by the knowledge that God has the power to renew your spirit and your life.

Are you in need of a new beginning? If so, turn your heart toward God in prayer. Are you weak or worried? Take the time—or, more accurately, make the time—to delve deeply into God's Holy Word. Are you spiritually depleted? Call upon fellow believers to support you, and call upon Christ to renew your sense of joy and thanksgiving. When you do, you'll discover that the Creator of the universe is in the business of making all things new—including you.

Working for Wisdom

Wisdom is a tree of life to those who embrace her; happy are those who hold her tightly.

All of us would like to be wise, but not all of us are willing to do the work that is required to become wise. Wisdom is not like a mushroom; it does not spring up overnight. It is, instead, like an oak tree that starts as a tiny acorn, grows into a sapling, and eventually reaches up to the sky, tall and strong.

To become wise, we must seek God's wisdom and live according to His Word. To become wise, we must seek wisdom with consistency and purpose. To become wise, we must not only learn the lessons of life, we must live by them.

Do you seek wisdom for yourself and for your family? Then keep learning and keep motivating your family members to do likewise. The ultimate source of wisdom, of course, is the Word of God. When you study God's Word and live according to His commandments, you will become wise . . . and you will be a blessing to your family and to the world.

Knowledge can be found in books or in school. Wisdom, on the other hand, starts with God . . . and ends there.

MARIE T. FREEMAN

Your Good Works

In the same way faith, if it doesn't have works, is dead by itself.

The central message of James' letter is the need for believers to act upon their beliefs. James' instruction is clear: "faith without works is dead." We are saved by our faith in Christ, but salvation does not signal the end of our earthly responsibilities; it marks the true beginning of our work for the Lord.

If your faith in God is strong, you will find yourself drawn toward God's work. You will serve Him, not just with words or prayers, but also with deeds. Because of your faith, you will feel compelled to do God's work—to do it gladly, faithfully, joyfully, and consistently.

Today, redouble your efforts to do God's bidding here on earth. Never have the needs—or the opportunities—been greater.

Ordinary work, which is what most of us do most of the time, is ordained by God every bit as much as is the extraordinary.

ELISABETH ELLIOT

Obedience and Peace

Those who love Your law have great peace, and nothing causes them to stumble.

PSALM 119:165 NASB

If we trust God's Word and live by it, we are blessed. But, if we choose to ignore God's commandments, the results are as predictable as they are tragic.

Life is a series of decisions and choices. Each day, we make countless decisions that can bring us closer to God . . . or not. When we live according to God's commandments, we earn the abundance and peace that He intends for our lives. But, when we distance ourselves from God, we rob ourselves of His precious gifts.

Do you seek God's peace and His blessings? Then obey Him. When you're faced with a difficult choice or a powerful temptation, seek God's counsel and trust the counsel He gives. Invite God into your heart and live according to His commandments. When you do, you will be blessed today, and tomorrow, and forever.

Obedience invites Christ to show his incomparable strength in our mortal weakness.

BETH MOORE

Happiness Now

For the happy heart, life is a continual feast.

PROVERBS 15:15 NLT

Happiness depends less upon our circumstances than upon our thoughts. When we turn our thoughts to God, to His gifts, and to His glorious creation, we experience the joy that God intends for His children. But, when we focus on the negative aspects of life, we suffer needlessly.

Do you sincerely want to be a happy Christian? Then set your mind and your heart upon God's love and His grace. The fullness of life in Christ is available to all who seek it and claim it. Count yourself among that number. Seek first the salvation that is available through a personal relationship with Jesus Christ, and then claim the joy, the peace, and the spiritual abundance that the Shepherd offers His sheep.

When we are set free from the bondage of pleasing others, when we are free from currying others' favor and others' approval—then no one will be able to make us miserable or dissatisfied. And then, if we know we have pleased God, contentment will be our consolation.

KAY ARTHUR

He Heals the Brokenhearted

God blesses the people who patiently endure testing. Afterward they will receive the crown of life that God has promised to those who love him.

JAMES 1:12 NLT

Women of every generation have experienced adversity, and this generation is no different. But, today's women face challenges that previous generations could have scarcely imagined. Thankfully, although the world continues to change, God's love remains constant. And, He remains ready to comfort us and strengthen us whenever we turn to Him.

Psalm 147 promises, "He heals the brokenhearted, and binds their wounds" (v. 3). When we are troubled, we must call upon God, and, in His own time and according to His own plan, He will heal us.

If you are like most women, it is simply a fact of life: from time to time, you worry. You worry about health, about finances, about safety, about relationships, about family, and about countless other challenges of life, some great and some small. Where is the best place to take your worries? Take them to God. Take your troubles to Him, and your fears, and your sorrows. Seek protection from the One who cannot be moved.

The Appropriate Response to Evil

So rid yourselves of all wickedness, all deceit, hypocrisy, envy, and all slander.

1 PETER 2:1 HCSB

Sometimes, anger can be a good thing. In the 21st chapter of Matthew, we are told how Christ responded when He confronted the evildoings of those who had invaded His Father's house of worship: "Then Jesus went into the temple of God and drove out all those who bought and sold in the temple, and overturned the tables of the money changers and the seats of those who sold doves. And He said to them, 'It is written, "My house shall be called a house of prayer," but you have made it a 'den of thieves'"" (vv. 12-13 NKJV). Thus Jesus demonstrated that righteous indignation is an appropriate response to evil.

When you come face-to-face with the devil's handiwork, don't be satisfied to remain safely on the sidelines. Instead, follow in the footsteps of your Savior. Jesus never compromised with evil, and neither should you.

Don't condone what God condemns.

ANONYMOUS

Beyond Blame

Get rid of all bitterness, rage, anger, harsh words, and slander, as well as all types of malicious behavior.

EPHESIANS 4:31 NLT

To blame others for our own problems is the height of futility. Yet blaming others is a favorite human pastime. Why? Because blaming is much easier than fixing, and criticizing others is so much easier than improving ourselves. So instead of solving our problems legitimately (by doing the work required to solve them) we are inclined to fret, to blame, and to criticize, while doing precious little else. When we do, our problems, quite predictably, remain unsolved.

Have you acquired the bad habit of blaming others for problems that you could or should solve yourself? If so, you are not only disobeying God's Word, you are also wasting your own precious time. So, instead of looking for someone to blame, look for something to fix, and then get busy fixing it. And as you consider your own situation, remember this: God has a way of helping those who help themselves, but He doesn't spend much time helping those who don't.

When It's Hard to Be Cheerful

*Be cheerful. Keep things in good repair. Keep your spirits
up. Think in harmony. Be agreeable. Do all that, and the
God of love and peace will be with you for sure.*

2 CORINTHIANS 13:11 MSG

O n some days, as every woman knows, it's hard to
be cheerful. Sometimes, as the demands of the
world increase and our energy sags, we feel less like
"cheering up" and more like "tearing up." But even in
our darkest hours, we can turn to God, and He will give
us comfort.

Few things in life are more sad, or, for that matter,
more absurd, than a grumpy Christian. Christ promises
us lives of abundance and joy, but He does not force
His joy upon us. We must claim His joy for ourselves,
and when we do, Jesus, in turn, fills our spirits with His
power and His love.

When we earnestly commit ourselves to the Savior
of mankind, when we place Jesus at the center of our
lives and trust Him as our personal Savior, He will
transform us, not just for today, but for all eternity.
Then we, as God's children, can share Christ's joy and
His message with a world that needs both.

Threatened by the Storms of Life

But Jesus quickly spoke to them, "Have courage! It is I. Do not be afraid."

MATTHEW 14:27 NCV

A storm rose quickly on the Sea of Galilee, and the disciples were afraid. Although they had seen Jesus perform many miracles, the disciples feared for their lives, so they turned to their Savior, and He calmed the waters and the wind.

Sometimes, we, like the disciples, feel threatened by the inevitable storms of life. And when we are fearful, we, too, can turn to Christ for courage and for comfort.

The next time you're afraid, remember that the One who calmed the wind and the waves is also your personal Savior. And remember that the ultimate battle has already been won at Calvary. We, as believers, can live courageously in the promises of our Lord...and we should.

When once we are assured that God is good, then there can be nothing left to fear.

HANNAH WHITALL SMITH

Beyond Doubt

Now if any of you lacks wisdom, he should ask God, who gives to all generously and without criticizing, and it will be given to him. But let him ask in faith without doubting. For the doubter is like the surging sea, driven and tossed by the wind.

JAMES 1:5-6 HCSB

If you've never had any doubts about your faith, then you can stop reading this page now and skip to the next. But if you've ever been plagued by doubts about your faith or your God, keep reading.

Even some of the most faithful Christians are, at times, beset by occasional bouts of discouragement and doubt. But even when we feel far removed from God, God is never far removed from us. He is always with us, always willing to calm the storms of life—always willing to replace our doubts with comfort and assurance.

Whenever you're plagued by doubts, that's precisely the moment you should seek God's presence by genuinely seeking to establish a deeper, more meaningful relationship with His Son. Then you may rest assured that in time, God will calm your fears, answer your prayers, and restore your confidence.

Your Eternal Journey

For God so loved the world that He gave His only begotten Son, that whoever believes in Him should not perish but have everlasting life.

JOHN 3:16 NKJV

Eternal life is not an event that begins when you die. Eternal life begins when you invite Jesus into your heart right here on earth. So it's important to remember that God's plans for you are not limited to the ups and downs of everyday life. If you've allowed Jesus to reign over your heart, you've already begun your eternal journey.

As mere mortals, our vision for the future, like our lives here on earth, is limited. God's vision is not burdened by such limitations: His plans extend throughout all eternity.

Let us praise the Creator for His priceless gift, and let us share the Good News with all who cross our paths. We return our Father's love by accepting His grace and by sharing His message and His love. When we do, we are blessed here on earth and throughout all eternity.

It is in giving that we receive, it is in pardoning that we are pardoned, it is in dying that we are born to eternal life.

ST. FRANCIS

A Healthy Fear

The fear of man brings a snare, but whoever trusts in the Lord shall be safe.

PROVERBS 29:25 NKJV

Are you a woman who possesses a healthy, fearful respect for God's power? Hopefully so. After all, God's Word teaches that the fear of the Lord is the beginning of knowledge (Proverbs 1:7).

When we fear the Creator—and when we honor Him by obeying His commandments—we receive God's approval and His blessings. But, when we ignore Him or disobey His commandments, we invite disastrous consequences.

God's hand shapes the universe, and it shapes our lives. God maintains absolute sovereignty over His creation, and His power is beyond comprehension. As believers, we must cultivate a sincere respect for God's awesome power. The fear of the Lord is, indeed, the beginning of knowledge. So today, as you face the realities of everyday life, remember this: until you acquire a healthy, respectful fear of God's power, your education is incomplete, and so is your faith.

You may not always see immediate results, but all God wants is your obedience and faithfulness.

VONETTE BRIGHT

Forgiveness and the Golden Rule

Therefore, whatever you want others to do for you, do also the same for them—this is the Law and the Prophets.

MATTHEW 7:12 HCSB

How should we treat other people? God's Word is clear: we should treat others in the same way that we wish to be treated. This Golden Rule is easy to understand but, at times, difficult to live by.

Because we are imperfect human beings, we are, on occasion, selfish, thoughtless, unforgiving, or even cruel. God commands us to behave otherwise. He teaches us to rise above our own imperfections and to treat others with mercy and compassion. When we observe God's Golden Rule, we help build His kingdom here on earth.

The words of Matthew 7:12 remind us that, as believers in Christ, we are commanded to forgive others just as we wish to be forgiven by them. This commandment is, indeed, the Golden Rule for Christians of every generation. When we weave the thread of forgiveness into the very fabric of our lives, we give glory to the One who first forgave us.

Don't put a question mark where God put a period.

ANONYMOUS

His Perfection

For I will proclaim the Lord's name. Declare the greatness of our God! The Rock—His work is perfect; all His ways are entirely just. A faithful God, without prejudice, He is righteous and true.

DEUTERONOMY 32:3-4 HCSB

The hand of God is perfect. God is the Creator of life, the Sustainer of life, and the Rock upon which righteous lives are built. God is a never-ending source of support for those who trust Him, and He is a never-ending source of wisdom for those who study His Holy Word.

Is God the Rock upon which you've constructed your own life? If so, then you have chosen wisely. Your faith will give you the inner strength you need to rise above the inevitable demands and struggles of life-here-on-earth.

God will hold your hand and walk with you today and every day if you let Him. Even if your circumstances are difficult, trust the Father. His promises remain true; His plan is perfect; His love is eternal; and His goodness endures forever.

God's Guidance

The true children of God are those who let God's Spirit lead them.

ROMANS 8:14 NCV

The Bible promises that God will guide you if you let Him. Your job, of course, is to let Him. But sometimes, you will be tempted to do otherwise. Sometimes, you'll be tempted to go along with the crowd; other times, you'll be tempted to do things your way, not God's way. When you feel those temptations, resist them.

What will you allow to guide you through the coming day: your own desires (or, for that matter, the desires of your friends)? Or will you allow God to lead the way? The answer should be obvious. You should let God be your guide. When you entrust your life to Him completely and without reservation, God will give you the strength to meet any challenge, the courage to face any trial, and the wisdom to live in His righteousness. So trust Him today and seek His guidance. When you do, your next step will be the right one.

God's leading will never be contrary to His word.

VONETTE BRIGHT

Everywhere

The eyes of the Lord are in every place, keeping watch....
PROVERBS 15:3 NKJV

If God is everywhere, why does He sometimes seem so far away? The answer to that question, of course, has nothing to do with God and everything to do with us.

When we begin each day on our knees, in praise and worship to Him, God often seems very near indeed. But, if we ignore God's presence or—worse yet—rebel against it altogether, the world in which we live becomes a spiritual wasteland.

Are you tired, discouraged or fearful? Be comforted because God is with you. Are you confused? Listen to the quiet voice of your Heavenly Father. Are you bitter? Talk with God and seek His guidance. Are you celebrating a great victory? Thank God and praise Him. He is the Giver of all things good.

In whatever condition you find yourself, wherever you are, whether you are happy or sad, victorious or vanquished, troubled or triumphant, celebrate God's presence. And be comforted. God is not just near. He is here.

He Provides

The Lord is my rock and my fortress and my deliverer; the God of my strength, in whom I will trust.

2 Samuel 22:2-3 NKJV

As a busy woman, you know from firsthand experience that life is not always easy. But as a recipient of God's grace, you also know that you are protected by a loving Heavenly Father.

In times of trouble, God will comfort you; in times of sorrow, He will dry your tears. When you are troubled, or weak, or sorrowful, God is neither distant nor disinterested. To the contrary, God is always present and always vitally engaged in the events of your life. Reach out to Him, and build your future on the rock that cannot be shaken . . . trust in God and rely upon His provisions. He can provide everything you really need . . . and far, far more.

Kept by His power—that is the only safety.

Oswald Chambers

The Will of God will never take you where the Grace of God will not protect you.

Anonymous

Your Hope, Your Confidence

Lord, I turn my hope to You. My God, I trust in You.
PSALM 25:1-2 HCSB

The hope that the world offers is fleeting and imperfect. The hope that God offers is unchanging, unshakable, and unending. It is no wonder, then, that when we seek security from worldly sources, our hopes are often dashed. Thankfully, God has no such record of failure.

Where will you place your hopes today? Will you entrust your future to man or to God? Will you seek solace exclusively from fallible human beings, or will you place your hopes, first and foremost, in the trusting hands of your Creator? The decision is yours, and you must live with the results of the choice you make.

For thoughtful believers, hope begins with God. Period. So today, as you embark upon the next stage of your life's journey, consider the words of the Psalmist: "You are my hope; O Lord GOD, You are my confidence" (71:5 NASB). Then, place your trust in the One who cannot be shaken.

The only hope we have is the only hope we've ever had.
ANGELA THOMAS

Judge Not

You, therefore, have no excuse, you who pass judgment on someone else, for at whatever point you judge the other, you are condemning yourself.

ROMANS 2:1 NIV

The warning of Matthew 7:1 is clear: "Judge not, that ye be not judged" (KJV). Yet even the most devoted Christians may fall prey to a powerful yet subtle temptation: the temptation to judge others. But as obedient followers of Christ, we are commanded to refrain from such behavior.

As Jesus came upon a young woman who had been condemned by the Pharisees, He spoke not only to the crowd that was gathered there, but also to all generations when He warned, "He that is without sin among you, let him first cast a stone at her" (John 8:7 KJV). Christ's message is clear, and it applies not only to the Pharisees of ancient times, but also to us.

Only Christ can free us from the prison of legalism, and then only if we are willing to be freed.

MADELEINE L'ENGLE

God Above Possessions

No one can serve two masters. The person will hate one master and love the other, or will follow one master and refuse to follow the other. You cannot serve both God and worldly riches.

MATTHEW 6:24 NCV

In our modern society, we need money to live. But as Christians, we must never make the acquisition of money the central focus of our lives. Money is a tool, but it should never overwhelm our sensibilities. The focus of life must be squarely on things spiritual, not things material.

Whenever we place our love for material possessions above our love for God—or when we yield to the countless other temptations of everyday living—we find ourselves engaged in a struggle between good and evil. Let us respond to this struggle by freeing ourselves from that subtle yet powerful temptation: the temptation to love the world more than we love God.

As faithful stewards of what we have, ought we not to give earnest thought to our staggering surplus?

ELISABETH ELLIOT

At Peace with the Past

Abundant peace belongs to those who love Your instruction; nothing makes them stumble.

PSALM 119:165 HCSB

Peace and bitterness are mutually exclusive. So, if you are mired in the quicksand of regret, it's time to plan your escape. How can you do so? By accepting the past.

The world holds few if any rewards for those who remain angrily focused upon the injustices of yesterday. Still, the act of forgiveness is difficult for all but the most saintly men and women. Being frail, fallible, imperfect human beings, most of us are quick to anger, quick to blame, slow to forgive, and even slower to forget. Yet as Christians, we are commanded to forgive others, just as we, too, have been forgiven.

If you have not yet made peace with the past, it's now time to declare an end to all hostilities. When you do so, you can then learn to live quite contentedly in a much more appropriate time period: this one.

We need to be at peace with our past, content with our present, and sure about our future, knowing they are all in God's hands.

JOYCE MEYER

Peace and His Word

Great peace have they which love thy law.

PSALM 119:165 KJV

Do you seek God's peace? Then study His Word. God's Word is unlike any other book. The Bible is a roadmap for life here on earth and for life eternal. As Christians, we are called upon to study God's Holy Word, to trust His Word, to follow its commandments, and to share its Good News with the world.

The words of Matthew 4:4 remind us that, "Man shall not live by bread alone but by every word that proceedeth out of the mouth of God" (KJV). As believers, we must study the Bible and meditate upon its meaning for our lives. Otherwise, we deprive ourselves of a priceless gift from our Creator.

Warren Wiersbe observed, "When the child of God looks into the Word of God, he sees the Son of God. And, he is transformed by the Spirit of God to share in the glory of God." God's Holy Word is, indeed, a transforming, life-changing, one-of-a-kind treasure. And, a passing acquaintance with the Good Book is insufficient for Christians who seek to obey God's Word and to understand His will. After all, man does not live by bread alone . . .

Too Much Stuff?

Keep your lives free from the love of money, and be satisfied with what you have.

HEBREWS 13:5 NCV

Okay, be honest—are you in love with stuff? If so, you're headed for trouble, and fast. Why? Because no matter how much you love stuff, stuff won't love you back.

In the life of committed Christians, material possessions should play a rather small role. Of course, we all need the basic necessities of life, but once we meet those needs for ourselves and for our families, the piling up of possessions creates more problems than it solves. Our real riches, of course, are not of this world. We are never really rich until we are rich in spirit.

Do you find yourself wrapped up in the concerns of the material world? If so, it's time to reorder your priorities by turning your thoughts and your prayers to more important matters. And, it's time to begin storing up riches that will endure throughout eternity: the spiritual kind.

I've learned to hold everything loosely because it hurts when God pries my fingers from it.

CORRIE TEN BOOM

He Deserves Your Best

For each tree is known by its own fruit.

LUKE 6:44 HCSB

God deserves your best. Is He getting it? Do you make an appointment with your Heavenly Father each day? Do you carve out moments when He receives your undivided attention? Or is your devotion to Him fleeting, distracted, and sporadic?

When you acquire the habit of focusing your heart and mind squarely upon God's intentions for your life, He will guide your steps and bless your endeavors. But if you allow distractions to take priority over your relationship with God, they will—and you will pay a price for your mistaken priorities.

Today, focus upon God's Word and upon His will for your life. When you do, you'll be amazed at how quickly everything else comes into focus, too.

Forgetting your mission leads, inevitably, to getting tangled up in details—details that can take you completely off your path.

LAURIE BETH JONES

Real Repentance

Come back to the LORD and live!

AMOS 5:6 NLT

Genuine repentance requires more than simply offering God apologies for our misdeeds. Real repentance may start with feelings of sorrow and remorse, but it ends only when we turn away from the sin that has heretofore distanced us from our Creator. In truth, we offer our most meaningful apologies to God, not with our words, but with our actions. As long as we are still engaged in sin, we may be "repenting," but we have not fully "repented."

Is there an aspect of your life that is distancing you from your God? If so, ask for His forgiveness, and—just as importantly—stop sinning. Then, wrap yourself in the protection of God's Word. When you do, you will be secure.

Before we can be filled with the Living Water, we must be cleansed of sin. Before we can be cleansed of sin, we must be convicted. And sometimes it's painful. And shameful.

ANNE GRAHAM LOTZ

The Power of Silence

Truly my soul silently waits for God; from Him comes my salvation.

PSALM 62:1 NKJV

Do you take time each day for an extended period of silence? And during those precious moments, do you sincerely open your heart to your Creator? If so, you are wise and you are blessed.

The world can be a noisy place, a place filled to the brim with distractions, interruptions, and frustrations. And if you're not careful, the struggles and stresses of everyday living can rob you of the peace that should rightfully be yours because of your personal relationship with Christ. So take time each day to quietly commune with your Savior. When you do, those moments of silence will enable you to participate more fully in the only source of peace that endures: God's peace.

Instead of waiting for the feeling, wait upon God. You can do this by growing still and quiet, then expressing in prayer what your mind knows is true about Him, even if your heart doesn't feel it at this moment.

SHIRLEY DOBSON

Defining Success

If you do not stand firm in your faith, then you will not stand at all.

ISAIAH 7:9 HCSB

How do you define success? Do you define it as the accumulation of material possessions or the adulation of your neighbors? If so, you need to reorder your priorities. Genuine success has little to do with fame or fortune; it has everything to do with God's gift of love and His promise of salvation.

If you have accepted Christ as your personal Savior, you are already a towering success in the eyes of God, but there is still more that you can do. Your task—as a believer who has been touched by the Creator's grace—is to accept the spiritual abundance and peace that He offers through the person of His Son. Then, you can share the healing message of God's love and His abundance with a world that desperately needs both. When you do, you have reached the pinnacle of success.

God's never been guilty of sponsoring a flop.

ETHEL WATERS

Focusing on Your Hopes

*This hope we have as an anchor of the soul, both sure and
steadfast, and which enters the Presence behind the veil.*

HEBREWS 6:19 NKJV

Paul Valéry observed, "We hope vaguely but dread
precisely." How true. All too often, we allow the
worries of everyday life to overwhelm our thoughts and
cloud our vision. What's needed is clearer perspective,
renewed faith, and a different focus.

When we focus on the frustrations of today or the
uncertainties of tomorrow, we rob ourselves of peace in
the present moment. But, when we focus on God's grace,
and when we trust in the ultimate wisdom of God's plan
for our lives, our worries no longer tyrannize us.

Today, remember that God is infinitely greater
than the challenges that you face. Remember also that
your thoughts are profoundly powerful, so guard them
accordingly.

As we have by faith said no to sin, so we should by faith
say yes to God and set our minds on things above, where
Christ is seated in the heavenlies.

VONETTE BRIGHT

Actions Speak Louder

Are there those among you who are truly wise and understanding? Then they should show it by living right and doing good things with a gentleness that comes from wisdom.

JAMES 3:13 NCV

The old saying is both familiar and true: actions speak louder than words. And as believers, we must beware: our actions should always give credence to the changes that Christ can make in the lives of those who walk with Him.

God calls upon each of us to act in accordance with His will and with respect for His commandments. If we are to be responsible believers, we must realize that it is never enough simply to hear the instructions of God; we must also live by them. And it is never enough to wait idly by while others do God's work here on earth; we, too, must act. Doing God's work is a responsibility that each of us must bear, and when we do, our loving Heavenly Father rewards our efforts with a bountiful harvest.

We set the sail; God makes the wind.

ANONYMOUS

Your Reasons to Rejoice

Keep your eyes focused on what is right, and look straight ahead to what is good.

PROVERBS 4:25 NCV

As a Christian woman, you have every reason to rejoice. God is in His heaven; Christ has risen, and dawn has broken on another day of life. But, when the demands of life seem great, you may find yourself feeling exhausted, discouraged, or both. That's when you need a fresh supply of hope . . . and God is ready, willing, and able to supply it.

The advice contained in Proverbs 4:5 is clear-cut: "Keep your eyes focused on what is right, and look straight ahead to what is good" (NCV). That's why you strive to maintain a positive, can-do attitude—an attitude that pleases God.

As you face the challenges of the coming day, use God's Word as a tool for directing your thoughts. When you do, your attitude will be pleasing to God, pleasing to your friends, and pleasing to yourself.

I could go through this day oblivious to the miracles all around me, or I could tune in and "enjoy."

GLORIA GAITHER

Celebrating His Gifts

Rejoice, and be exceeding glad: for great is your reward in heaven . . . .

MATTHEW 5:12 KJV

Do you celebrate the gifts God has given you? Do you pray without ceasing? Do you rejoice in the beauty of God's glorious creation? You should. But perhaps, as a busy woman living in a demanding world, you have been slow to count your gifts and even slower to give thanks to the Giver.

As God's children, we are all blessed beyond measure, and we should celebrate His blessings every day that we live. The gifts we receive from God are multiplied when we share them with others. Today is a non-renewable resource—once it's gone, it's gone forever. Our responsibility—as believers—is to give thanks for God's gifts and then use them in the service of God's will and in the service of His people.

God has blessed us beyond measure, and we owe Him everything, including our praise. And let us remember that for those of us who have been saved by God's only begotten Son, every day is a cause for celebration.

Comforting Others

Blessed be the God and Father of our Lord Jesus Christ, the Father of mercies and the God of all comfort. He comforts us in all our affliction, so that we may be able to comfort those who are in any kind of affliction, through the comfort we ourselves receive from God.

2 CORINTHIANS 1:3-4 HCSB

The 118th Psalm reminds us, "This is the day which the Lord hath made; we will rejoice and be glad in it" (v. 24 KJV). As we rejoice in this day that the Lord has given us, let us remember that an important part of today's celebration is the time we spend comforting those in need.

Each day provides countless opportunities to encourage others and to assist those who need our help. When we do, we spread seeds of hope and happiness.

Today, when you encounter someone who needs a helping hand or a comforting word, be generous with both. You possess the power to make the world a better place one person—and one hug—at a time. When you use that power wisely, you make your own corner of the world a kinder, gentler, happier place.

Facing Difficult Days

We are pressured in every way but not crushed; we are perplexed but not in despair.

2 CORINTHIANS 4:8 HCSB

All of us face difficult days. Sometimes even the most devout Christian women can become discouraged, and you are no exception. After all, you live in a world where expectations can be high and demands can be even higher.

If you find yourself enduring difficult circumstances, remember that God remains in His heaven. If you become discouraged with the direction of your day or your life, turn your thoughts and prayers to Him. He is a God of possibility, not negativity. He will guide you through your difficulties and beyond them. And then, with a renewed spirit of optimism and hope, you can thank the Giver of all things good for gifts that are simply too numerous to count.

When life is difficult, God wants us to have a faith that trusts and waits.

KAY ARTHUR

A Beacon of Encouragement

Encourage each other. Live in harmony and peace. Then the God of love and peace will be with you.

2 CORINTHIANS 13:11 NLT

One of the reasons that God placed you here on earth is so that you might become a beacon of encouragement to the world. As a faithful follower of the One from Galilee, you have every reason to be hopeful, and you have every reason to share your hopes with others. When you do, you will discover that hope, like other human emotions, is contagious.

As a follower of Christ, you are instructed to choose your words carefully so as to build others up through wholesome, honest encouragement (Ephesians 4:29). So look for the good in others and celebrate the good that you find. As the old saying goes, "When someone does something good, applaud—you'll make two people happy."

Giving encouragement to others is a most welcome gift, for the results of it are lifted spirits, increased self-worth, and a hopeful future.

FLORENCE LITTAUER

Faith That Works

For in the gospel a righteousness from God is revealed, a righteousness that is by faith from first to last, just as it is written: "The righteous will live by faith."

ROMANS 1:17 NIV

Through every stage of your life, God stands by your side, ready to strengthen you and protect you . . . if you have faith in Him. When you place your faith, your trust, indeed your life in the hands of Christ Jesus, you'll be amazed at the marvelous things He can do with you and through you.

So make this promise to yourself and keep it: make certain that your faith is a faith that works. How? You can strengthen your faith through praise, through worship, through Bible study, and through prayer. When you do so, you'll learn to trust God's plans. With Him, all things are possible, and He stands ready to open a world of possibilities to you . . . if you have faith.

Faith is not just believing; faith is being open to what God is doing, being willing to learn and grow.

MARY MORRISON SUGGS

Forgiveness Now

Anyone who claims to live in God's light and hates a brother or sister is still in the dark.

1 JOHN 2:9 MSG

Forgiveness is seldom easy, but it is always right. When we forgive those who have hurt us, we honor God by obeying His commandments. But when we harbor bitterness against others, we disobey God—with predictably unhappy results.

Are you easily frustrated by the inevitable shortcomings of others? Are you a prisoner of bitterness or regret? If so, perhaps you need a refresher course in the art of forgiveness.

If there exists even one person, alive or dead, whom you have not forgiven (and that includes yourself), follow God's commandment and His will for your life: forgive that person today. And remember that bitterness, anger, and regret are not part of God's plan for your life. Forgiveness is.

If Jesus forgave those who nailed Him to the Cross, and if God forgives you and me, how can you withhold your forgiveness from someone else?

ANNE GRAHAM LOTZ

Teaching Generosity

Teach a youth about the way he should go; even when he is old he will not depart from it.

PROVERBS 22:6 HCSB

God rewards generosity just as surely as He punishes sin. If we become "generous souls" in the service of our Lord, God blesses us in ways that we cannot fully understand. But if we allow ourselves to become closefisted and miserly, either with our possessions or with our love, we deprive ourselves of the spiritual abundance that would otherwise be ours.

Do you seek God's abundance and His peace? Then share the blessings that God has given you—and teach your family members to do likewise. Share your possessions, share your faith, share your testimony, and share your love. God expects no less, and He deserves no less. And neither, come to think of it, do your neighbors.

If we can learn to develop a giving heart toward those in our own homes and families, we'll be much more free to give ungrudgingly—and at the Spirit's prompting—to those in the most desperate need.

MARY HUNT

His Wondrous Handiwork

Then God saw everything that He had made, and indeed it was very good.

GENESIS 1:31 NKJV

As we pause to examine God's wondrous handiwork, one thing is clear: God is, indeed, a miracle worker. Throughout history He has intervened in the course of human events in ways which can't be explained by science or human rationale.

God's miracles are not limited to special occasions, nor are they witnessed by a select few. God is crafting His wonders all around us: the miracle of the birth of a new baby; the miracle of a world renewing itself with every sunrise; the miracle of lives transformed by God's love and by His grace. Each day God's miraculous handiwork is evident for all to see and to experience.

The Psalmist reminds us that the heavens are a declaration of God's glory. May we never cease to praise the Father for a universe that stands as an awesome testimony to His presence, to His power, and to His love.

You are God's chief creation, and you are here for His pleasure and His glory.

BETH MOORE

He Is Love

God is love, and the one who remains in love remains in God, and God remains in him.

1 John 4:16 HCSB

God is love. It's a sweeping statement, a profoundly important description of what God is and how God works. God's love is perfect. When we open our hearts to His perfect love, we are touched by the Creator's hand, and we are transformed.

Barbara Johnson observed, "We cannot protect ourselves from trouble, but we can dance through the puddles of life with a rainbow smile, twirling the only umbrella we need—the umbrella of God's love."

And the English mystical writer Juliana of Norwich noted, "We are so preciously loved by God that we cannot even comprehend it. No created being can ever know how much and how sweetly and tenderly God loves them."

So today, even if you can only carve out a few quiet moments, offer sincere prayers of thanksgiving to your Father. Thank Him for His blessings and His love.

Love has its source in God, for love is the very essence of His being.

KAY ARTHUR

Demonstrating Our Love

And God is able to make every grace overflow to you, so that in every way, always having everything you need, you may excel in every good work.

2 Corinthians 9:8 HCSB

How can we demonstrate our love for God? By accepting His Son as our personal Savior and by placing Him at the very center of our lives. Jesus said that if we are to love Him, we must obey His commandments. Thus, obedience to the Master is an expression of love.

In Ephesians 2:10 we read, "For we are His workmanship, created in Christ Jesus for good works, which God prepared beforehand that we should walk in them." These words instruct us that we are not saved by good works, but for good works. Good works are not the root, but rather the fruit of our salvation.

Today and every day, let the fruits of your stewardship be a clear demonstration of your love for Christ. He has given you spiritual abundance and eternal life. You, in turn, owe Him your obedience and your love.

Hands are made for work, and the heart is made for God.

Josepha Rossello

Beyond Jealousy

Where jealousy and selfishness are, there will be confusion and every kind of evil.

JAMES 3:14 NCV

Are you too wise to be consumed with feelings of jealousy? Hopefully so. After all, Jesus clearly taught us to love our neighbors, not to envy them. But sometimes, despite our best intentions, we fall prey to feelings of resentfulness, jealousy, bitterness, and envy. Why? Because we are human, and because we live in a world that places great importance on material possessions (possessions which, by the way, are totally unimportant to God).

The next time you feel pangs of envy invading your thoughts, remind yourself of two things: 1. Envy is a sin, and 2. God has already showered you with so many blessings that if you're a thoughtful, thankful believer, you have no right to ever be envious of any other person on earth.

What God asks, does, or requires of others is not my business; it is His.

KAY ARTHUR

Preparing for Eternity

These things I have written to you who believe in the name of the Son of God, that you may know that you have eternal life.

1 JOHN 5:13 NKJV

God has given you the gift of life. How will you use that gift? Will you allow God's Son to reign over your heart? And will you treat each day as a precious treasure from your Heavenly Father? You should, and, hopefully, you will.

Every day that we live, we should be preparing to die. If we seek to live purposeful, productive lives, we will be ever mindful that our time here on earth is limited, and we will conduct ourselves accordingly.

Life is a glorious opportunity, but it is also shockingly brief. We must serve God each day as if it were our last day. When we do, we prepare ourselves for the inevitable end of life here on earth, and the victory that is certain to follow.

You have a glorious future in Christ! Live every moment in His power and love.

VONETTE BRIGHT

The Wisdom of Moderation

Moderation is better than muscle, self-control better than political power.

PROVERBS 16:32 MSG

Moderation and wisdom are traveling companions. If we are wise, we must learn to temper our appetites, our desires, and our impulses. When we do, we are blessed, in part, because God has created a world in which temperance is rewarded and intemperance is inevitably punished.

Would you like to improve your life? Then harness your appetites and restrain your impulses. Moderation is difficult, of course; it is especially difficult in a prosperous society such as ours. But the rewards of moderation are numerous and long-lasting. Claim those rewards today.

No one can force you to moderate your appetites. The decision to live temperately (and wisely) is yours and yours alone. And so are the consequences.

Contentment has a way of quieting insatiable desires.

MARY HUNT

Giving Up?

*It is better to finish something than to start it. It is better
to be patient than to be proud.*

ECCLESIASTES 7:8 NCV

Occasional disappointments, detours, and failures
are inevitable, even for the most accomplished
among us. Setbacks are simply the price that we must
sometimes pay for our willingness to take risks as
we follow our dreams. But when we encounter these
hardships, we must never lose faith.

American children's rights advocate Marian Wright
Edelman asked, "Whoever said anybody has a right to
give up?" And that's a question that are most certainly
should ask yourself, especially when times get tough.

Are you willing to keep fighting the good fight even
when you meet unexpected difficulties? If you'll decide
to press on through temporary setbacks, you may soon
be surprised at the creative ways God finds to help
determined people like you—people who possess the
wisdom and the courage to persevere.

Are you a Christian? If you are, how can you be
hopeless?

ANNE GRAHAM LOTZ

The Antidote to Fear

I sought the LORD, and he heard me, and delivered me from all my fears.

PSALM 34:4 KJV

Considered by some to be the most popular cowgirl of time, she starred with cowboy husband Roy Rogers, and she wrote their theme song "Happy Trails." She was Dale Evans, and she said, "I have found the perfect antidote for fear. Whenever it sticks up its ugly face, I clobber it with prayer."

The Psalmist, said, "In my distress I prayed to the LORD, and the LORD answered me and rescued me" (118:5). And He'll do the same for you. So if you've been beset by the inevitable disappointments and fears that grip us all from time to time, pray for courage and keep praying. When you, then like Dale Evans and Roy Rogers, you'll see plenty of clear skies and lots of happy trails.

I need the spiritual revival that comes from spending quiet time alone with Jesus in prayer and in thoughtful meditation on His Word.

ANNE GRAHAM LOTZ

At Peace with Your Purpose

The Lord will work out his plans for my life—for your faithful love, O Lord, endures forever.

PSALM 138:8 NLT

Are you at peace with the direction of your life? If you're a Christian, you should be. Even if God's plans for you are uncertain, His love for you is not.

The familiar words of John 14:27 give us hope: "Peace I leave with you, My peace I give unto you . . . ." Jesus offers us peace, not as the world gives, but as He alone gives. We, as believers, can accept His peace or ignore it.

When we accept the peace of Jesus Christ into our hearts, our lives are transformed. And then, because we possess the gift of peace, we can share that gift with fellow believers, family members, friends, and associates. If, on the other hand, we choose to ignore the gift of peace—for whatever reason—we simply cannot share what we do not possess.

Today, as a gift to yourself, to your family, and to your friends, claim the inner peace that is your spiritual birthright: the peace of Jesus Christ. It is offered freely; it has been paid for in full; it is yours for the asking. So ask. And then share.

Embraced by Him

That is, in Christ, he chose us before the world was made so that we would be his holy people—people without blame before him. Because of his love, God had already decided to make us his own children through Jesus Christ. That was what he wanted and what pleased him,

EPHESIANS 1:4-5 NCV

Every day of our lives—indeed, every moment of our lives—we are embraced by God. He is always with us, and His love for us is deeper and more profound than we can imagine.

Gloria Gaither observed, "Being loved by Him whose opinion matters most gives us the security to risk loving, too—even loving ourselves."

And Lisa Whelchel had this advice: "Believing that you are loved will set you free to be who God created you to be. So rest in His love and just be yourself."

Let these words serve as a powerful reminder: you are a marvelous, glorious being, created by a loving God who wants you to become—completely and without reservation—the woman He created you to be.

Spiritual Gifts

Pursue love and desire spiritual gifts.

1 CORINTHIANS 14:1 HCSB

All of us have spiritual gifts, and if we're wise, we continue to refine those gifts every day. The journey toward spiritual maturity lasts a lifetime. As Christians, we can and should continue to grow in the love and the knowledge of our Savior as long as we live. When we cease to grow, either emotionally or spiritually, we do ourselves a profound disservice. But, if we study God's Word, if we obey His commandments, and if we live in the center of His will, we will not be "stagnant" believers; we will, instead, be growing Christians . . . and that's exactly what God intends for us to be.

Life is a series of choices and decisions. Each day, we make countless decisions that can bring us closer to God . . . or not. When we live according to the principles contained in God's Holy Word, we embark upon a journey of spiritual maturity that results in life abundant and life eternal.

If you want to discover your spiritual gifts, start obeying God. As you serve Him, you will find that He has given you the gifts that are necessary to follow through in obedience.

ANNE GRAHAM LOTZ

Which Path?

In all your ways acknowledge Him, and He shall direct your paths.

PROVERBS 3:6 NKJV

Each day, as we awaken from sleep, we are confronted with countless opportunities to serve God and to follow in the footsteps of His Son. When we do, our Heavenly Father guides our steps and blesses our endeavors.

As citizens of a fast-changing world, we face challenges that sometimes leave us feeling overworked, overcommitted, and overwhelmed. But God has different plans for us. He intends that we slow down long enough to praise Him and to glorify His Son. When we do, He lifts our spirits and enriches our lives.

Today provides a glorious opportunity to place yourself in the service of the One who is the Giver of all blessings. May you seek His will, may you trust His Word, and may you walk in the footsteps of His Son.

It is not the business of the church to adapt Christ to men, but men to Christ.

DOROTHY SAYERS

Trust Him

*And God, in his mighty power, will protect you until you
receive this salvation, because you are trusting him.*

1 PETER 1:5 NLT

Sometimes the future seems bright, and sometimes
it does not. Yet even when we cannot see the
possibilities of tomorrow, God can. As believers, our
challenge is to trust an uncertain future to an all-
powerful God.

When we trust God, we should trust Him without
reservation. We should steel ourselves against the
inevitable disappointments of the day, secure in the
knowledge that our Heavenly Father has a plan for the
future that only He can see.

Can you place your future into the hands of a
loving and all-knowing God? Can you live amid the
uncertainties of today, knowing that God has dominion
over all your tomorrows? If you can, you are wise and
you are blessed. When you trust God with everything
you are and everything you have, He will bless you now
and forever.

Out of Balance?

Happy is the person who finds wisdom and gains understanding.

Proverbs 3:13 NLT

Sometimes, amid the concerns of everyday life, we lose perspective. Life seems out of balance as we confront an array of demands that sap our strength and cloud our thoughts. What's needed is a renewed faith, a fresh perspective, and God's wisdom.

Here in the 21st century, commentary is commonplace and information is everywhere. But the ultimate source of wisdom, the kind of timeless wisdom that God willingly shares with His children, is still available from a single unique source: the Holy Bible.

The wisdom of the world changes with the ever-shifting sands of public opinion. God's wisdom does not. His wisdom is eternal. It never changes. And it most certainly is the wisdom that you must use to plan your day, your life, and your eternal destiny.

Seek wisdom. It's out there.

Sheila Walsh

The Treasure Hunt

For where your treasure is, there will your heart be also.

LUKE 12:34 KJV

All of mankind is engaged in a colossal, worldwide treasure hunt. Some people seek treasure from earthly sources, treasures such as material wealth or public acclaim; others seek God's treasures by making Him the cornerstone of their lives.

What kind of treasure hunter are you? Are you so caught up in the demands of everyday living that you sometimes allow the search for worldly treasures to become your primary focus? If so, it's time to reorganize your daily to-do list by placing God in His rightful place: first place. Don't allow anyone or anything to separate you from your Heavenly Father and His only begotten Son.

The world's treasures are difficult to find and difficult to keep; God's treasures are ever-present and everlasting. Which treasures, then, will you claim as your own?

I have a divided heart, trying to love God and the world at the same time. God says, "You can't love me as you should if you love this world too."

MARY MORRISON SUGGS

Excited About the Opportunities

May the God of hope fill you with all joy and peace as you trust in him, so that you may overflow with hope by the power of the Holy Spirit.

ROMANS 15:13 NIV

Are you excited about the opportunities of today and thrilled by the possibilities of tomorrow? Do you confidently expect God to lead you to a place of abundance, peace, and joy? And, when your days on earth are over, do you expect to receive the priceless gift of eternal life? If you trust God's promises, and if you have welcomed God's Son into your heart, then you believe that your future is intensely and eternally bright.

Today, as you prepare to meet the duties of everyday life, pause and consider God's promises. And then think for a moment about the wonderful future that awaits all believers, including you. God has promised that your future is secure. Trust that promise, and celebrate the life of abundance and eternal joy that is now yours through Christ.

Holiness Before Happiness

If they serve Him obediently, they will end their days in prosperity and their years in happiness.

JOB 36:11 HCSB

Because you are an imperfect human being, you are not "perfectly" happy—and that's perfectly okay with God. He is far less concerned with your happiness than He is with your holiness.

God continuously reveals Himself in everyday life, but He does not do so in order to make you contented; He does so in order to lead you to His Son. So don't be overly concerned with your current level of happiness: it will change. Be more concerned with the current state of your relationship with Christ: He does not change. And because your Savior transcends time and space, you can be comforted in the knowledge that in the end, His joy will become your joy . . . for all eternity.

His goal is not necessarily to make us happy. His goal is to make us His.

KATHY TROCCOLI

Christ is the secret, the source, the substance, the center, and the circumference of all true and lasting gladness.

MRS. CHARLES E. COWMAN

God's Abundance

*You did not choose me, but I chose you and appointed you
to go and bear fruit—fruit that will last. Then the Father
will give you whatever you ask in my name.*

JOHN 15:16 NIV

Do you seek God's abundance for yourself and
your family? Of course you do. And it's worth
remembering that God's rewards are most certainly
available to you and yours. The 10th chapter of John tells
us that Christ came to earth so that our lives might be
filled with abundance. But what, exactly, did Jesus mean
when He promised "life . . . more abundantly"? Was He
referring to material possessions or financial wealth?
Hardly. Jesus offers a different kind of abundance: a
spiritual richness that extends beyond the temporal
boundaries of this world. This everlasting abundance
is available to all who seek it and claim it. May you
and your family claim those riches, and may you share
Christ's blessings with all who cross your path.

If you want purpose and meaning and satisfaction and
fulfillment and peace and hope and joy and abundant
life that lasts forever, look to Jesus.

ANNE GRAHAM LOTZ

Beyond Panic

When my anxious thoughts multiply within me, Your consolations delight my soul.

PSALM 94:19 NASB

We live in a world that seems to invite panic. Everywhere we turn, or so it seems, we are confronted with disturbing images that seem to cry out. "All is lost." But with God, there is always hope.

God calls us to live above and beyond anxiety. God calls us to live by faith, not by fear. He instructs us to trust Him completely, this day and forever. But sometimes, trusting God is difficult, especially when we become caught up in the incessant demands of an anxious world.

When you feel anxious—and you will—return your thoughts to God's love. Then, take your concerns to Him in prayer and, to the best of your ability, leave them there. Whatever "it" is, God is big enough to handle it. Let Him . . . now!

Look around you and you'll be distressed; look within yourself and you'll be depressed; look at Jesus, and you'll be at rest!

CORRIE TEN BOOM

His Compassion

For thou, LORD, wilt bless the righteous . . . .

PSALM 5:12 KJV

Psalm 145 makes this promise: "The LORD is gracious and compassionate, slow to anger and rich in love. The LORD is good to all; he has compassion on all he has made" (vv. 8-9 NIV).

Most of us have been blessed beyond measure, but sometimes, as busy women living in a demanding world, we are sometimes slow to count our gifts and even slower to give thanks to the Giver. Our blessings include life and health, family and friends, freedom and possessions—for starters. And those blessings are multiplied when we share them with others.

As the old saying goes, "When we drink the water, we should remember the spring." May we, who have been so richly blessed, give thanks for our gifts—and may we demonstrate our gratitude by sharing them.

I discovered that sorrow was not to be feared but rather endured with hope and expectancy that God would use it to visit and bless my life.

JILL BRISCOE

Caring for Our Children

Then He took a child, had him stand among them, and taking him in His arms, He said to them, "Whoever welcomes one little child such as this in My name welcomes Me. And whoever welcomes Me does not welcome Me, but Him who sent Me."

MARK 9:36-37 HCSB

Have you hugged a child lately? If so, you've experienced one of life's great pleasures. Every child is a priceless gift from the Creator. And when we share love and affection with our children, we—and they—are blessed beyond measure.

As parents, friends of parents, aunts, and grandmothers, we understand the critical importance of raising our children with love, with discipline, and with God. It's a tall order and a profoundly important responsibility . . . but with God's help, we can do it.

Every child deserves the presence of caring adults who serve as godly role models. May we, as concerned adults, behave ourselves—and raise our children—accordingly.

Every child born into the world is a new thought of God, an ever-fresh and radiant possibility.

KATE DOUGLAS WIGGIN

Living Courageously

So do not fear, for I am with you; do not be dismayed, for I am your God. I will strengthen you and help you; I will uphold you with my righteous right hand.

ISAIAH 41:10 NIV

Christian women have every reason to live courageously. After all, the final battle has already been won on the cross at Calvary. But even dedicated followers of Christ may find their courage tested by the inevitable disappointments and fears that visit the lives of believers and non-believers alike.

When you find yourself worried about the challenges of today or the uncertainties of tomorrow, you must ask yourself whether or not you are ready to place your concerns and your life in God's all-powerful, all-knowing, all-loving hands. If the answer to that question is yes—as it should be—then you can draw courage today from the source of strength that never fails: your Heavenly Father.

Shall we be afraid to hide ourselves in the keeping power of our Divine Keeper, who neither slumbers nor sleeps, and who has promised to preserve our going out and our coming in, from this time forth and even forever more?

HANNAH WHITALL SMITH

God Never Leaves

No, I will not abandon you as orphans—I will come to you.

JOHN 14:18 NLT

Doubts come in several shapes and sizes: doubts about God, doubts about the future, and doubts about our own abilities, for starters. But when doubts creep in, as they will from time to time, we need not despair. As Sheila Walsh observed, "To wrestle with God does not mean that we have lost faith, but that we are fighting for it."

God never leaves our side, not for an instant. He is always with us, always willing to calm the storms of life. When we sincerely seek His presence—and when we genuinely seek to establish a deeper, more meaningful relationship Him—God is prepared to touch our hearts, to calm our fears, to answer our doubts, and to restore our confidence.

Just as I am, though tossed about with many a conflict, many a doubt, fightings and fears within, without, O Lamb of God, I come, I come.

CHARLOTTE ELLIOTT

Encouraging Words for Family and Friends

Do not let any unwholesome talk come out of your mouths, but only what is helpful for building others up according to their needs, that it may benefit those who listen.

EPHESIANS 4:29 NIV

Life is a team sport, and all of us need occasional pats on the back from our teammates. As Christians, we are called upon to spread the Good News of Christ, and we are also called to spread a message of encouragement and hope to the world.

Whether you realize it or not, many people with whom you come in contact every day are in desperate need of a smile or an encouraging word. The world can be a difficult place, and countless friends and family members may be troubled by the challenges of everyday life. Since you don't always know who needs our help, the best strategy is to try to encourage all the people who cross your path. So today, be a world-class source of encouragement to everyone you meet. Never has the need been greater.

My special friends, who know me so well and love me anyway, give me daily encouragement to keep on.

EMILIE BARNES

Facing Your Fears

They won't be afraid of bad news; their hearts are steady because they trust the Lord.

PSALM 112:7 NCV

Do you prefer to face your fears rather than run from them? If so, you will be blessed because of your willingness to live courageously.

When Paul wrote Timothy, he reminded his young protégé that the God they served was a bold God, and God's spirit empowered His children with boldness also. Like Timothy, we face times of uncertainty and fear. God's message is the same to us, today, as it was to Timothy: We can live boldly because the spirit of God resides in us.

So today, as you face the challenges of everyday living, remember that God is with you . . . and you are protected.

God knows that the strength that comes from wrestling with our fear will give us wings to fly.

PAULA RINEHART

Facing our deepest fears means making peace with our seen self and with our unseen self.

SHEILA WALSH

Forgiveness and Renewal

And whenever you stand praying, if you have anything against anyone, forgive him, so that your Father in heaven may also forgive you your wrongdoing.

MARK 11:25 HCSB

Bitterness saps your energy; genuine forgiveness renews your spirit. If you find yourself tired, discouraged, or worse, perhaps you need to ask God to help you forgive others (just as He has already forgiven you).

God intends that His children lead joyous lives filled with abundance and peace. But sometimes, abundance and peace seem very far away. It is in these dark moments that we must turn to God for renewal; when we do, He will restore us.

Are you embittered about the past? Turn your heart toward God in prayer. Are you spiritually depleted? Call upon fellow believers to support you, and call upon Christ to renew your spirit and your life. Do you sincerely want to forgive someone? Ask God to heal your heart. When you do, you'll discover that the Creator of the universe stands always ready and always able to create a new sense of wonderment and joy in you.

When We Cannot Understand

"For my thoughts are not your thoughts, neither are your ways my ways," declares the LORD. "As the heavens are higher than the earth, so are my ways higher than your ways and my thoughts than your thoughts."

ISAIAH 55:8-9 NIV

Try though we might, we simply cannot understand God. We can see His handiwork; we can feel His presence; we can worship His Son; but as mere mortals, we lack the capacity to comprehend a being of infinite power and infinite love. Someday, we will understand Him completely, but until then, we must trust Him completely.

The journey through life leads us over many peaks and through many valleys. When we reach the mountaintops, we find it easy to praise God, to trust Him, and to give thanks. But, when we trudge through the dark valleys of bitterness and despair, trusting God is more difficult.

When our courage is tested to the limit, we must lean upon God's promises. And we must remember that God rules both mountaintops and valleys—with limitless wisdom and unchanging love—now and forever.

He Will Instruct You

You will teach me how to live a holy life. Being with you will fill me with joy; at your right hand I will find pleasure forever.

PSALM 16:11 NCV

God has made this promise to you: He will instruct you in the way you should go. God is always willing to teach, and you should always be willing to learn . . . but sometimes, you will be tempted to ignore God's instruction. Don't do it—instead of ignoring God, start praying about your situation . . . and start listening!

When we sincerely offer heartfelt prayers to our Heavenly Father, He will give direction and meaning to our lives—but He won't force us to follow Him. To the contrary, God has given us the free will to follow His commandments, or not. When we stray from God's commandments, we invite bitter consequences. But, when we follow His commandments—and when we genuinely and humbly seek His instruction—God touches our hearts and leads us on the path of His choosing.

Will you trust God to teach you "in the way you should go"? Prayerfully, you will, because to do otherwise is not only the opposite of wisdom; it is also the prelude to disaster.

Setting Aside Quiet Moments

The Lord is with you when you are with Him. If you seek Him, He will be found by you.

2 CHRONICLES 15:2 HCSB

Since God is everywhere, we are free to sense His presence whenever we take the time to quiet our souls and turn our prayers to Him. But sometimes, amid the incessant demands of everyday life, we turn our thoughts far from God; when we do, we suffer.

Do you set aside quiet moments each day to offer praise to your Creator? As a woman who has received the gift of God's grace, you most certainly should. Silence is a gift that you give to yourself and to God. During these moments of stillness, you will often sense the infinite love and power of your Creator—and He, in turn, will speak directly to your heart.

The familiar words of Psalm 46:10 remind us to "Be still, and know that I am God." When we do so, we encounter the awesome presence of our loving Heavenly Father, and we are comforted in the knowledge that God is not just near. He is here.

God's Sovereignty

Can you solve the mysteries of God? Can you discover everything there is to know about the Almighty? Such knowledge is higher than the heavens—but who are you? It is deeper than the underworld—what can you know in comparison to him? It is broader than the earth and wider than the sea.

JOB 11:7-9 NLT

God is sovereign. He reigns over the entire universe and He reigns over your little corner of that universe. Your challenge is to recognize God's sovereignty and live in accordance with His commandments. Sometimes, of course, this is easier said than done.

Your Heavenly Father may not always reveal Himself as quickly (or as clearly) as you would like. But rest assured: God is in control, God is here, and God intends to use you in wonderful, unexpected ways. He desires to lead you along a path of His choosing. Your challenge is to watch, to listen, to learn . . . and to follow.

Waiting is the hardest kind of work, but God knows best, and we may joyfully leave all in His hands.

LOTTIE MOON

He Overcomes the World

God decided to let his people know this rich and glorious secret which he has for all people. This secret is Christ himself, who is in you. He is our only hope for glory.

COLOSSIANS 1:27 NCV

There are few sadder sights on earth than the sight of a person who has lost all hope. In difficult times, hope can be elusive, but Christians need never lose it. After all, God is good; His love endures; He has promised His children the gift of eternal life.

If you find yourself falling into the spiritual traps of worry and discouragement, consider the words of Jesus. It was Christ who promised, "In the world you will have tribulation; but be of good cheer, I have overcome the world" (John 16:33 NKJV). This world is, indeed, a place of trials and tribulations, but as believers, we are secure. God has promised us peace, joy, and eternal life. And, of course, God always keeps His promises.

In those desperate times when we feel like we don't have an ounce of strength, He will gently pick up our heads so that our eyes can behold something—something that will keep His hope alive in us.

KATHY TROCCOLI

Judging Others

Do not judge, or you too will be judged. For in the same way you judge others, you will be judged, and with the measure you use, it will be measured to you.

MATTHEW 7:1 NIV

We have all fallen short of God's commandments, and He has forgiven us. We, too, must forgive others. And, we must refrain from judging them.

Are you one of those people who finds it easy to judge others? If so, it's time to change.

God does not need (or, for that matter, want) your help. Why? Because God is perfectly capable of judging the human heart . . . while you are not.

As Christians, we are warned that to judge others is to invite fearful consequences: to the extent we judge others, so, too, will we be judged by God. Let us refrain, then, from judging our neighbors. Instead, let us forgive them and love them in the same way that God has forgiven us.

Media Messages

Don't become so well-adjusted to your culture that you fit into it without even thinking. Instead, fix your attention on God.

ROMANS 12:2 MSG

Sometimes it's hard being a woman of faith especially when the world keeps pumping out messages that are contrary to your beliefs.

Beware! The media is working around the clock in an attempt to rearrange your priorities. The media says that appearance is all-important, that thinness is all-important, and that social standing is all-important. But guess what? Those messages are untrue. The important things in life have little to do with appearances. The all-important things in life have to do with your faith, your family, and your future. Period.

Because you live in the 21st century, you are relentlessly bombarded by media messages that are contrary to your faith. Take those messages with a grain of salt—or better yet, don't take them at all.

We are made spiritually lethargic by a steady diet of materialism.

MARY MORRISON SUGGS

Acknowledging God's Sovereignty

However, I did give them this command: Obey Me, and then I will be your God, and you will be My people. You must walk in every way I command you so that it may go well with you.

JEREMIAH 7:23 HCSB

Proverbs 3:6 makes this promise: if you acknowledge God's sovereignty over every aspect of your life, He will guide your path. And, as you prayerfully consider the path that God intends for you to take, here are things you should do: You should study His Word and be ever-watchful for His signs. You should associate with fellow believers who will encourage your spiritual growth. You should listen carefully to that inner voice that speaks to you in the quiet moments of your daily devotionals. And, as you continually seek God's unfolding purpose for your life, you should be patient. Your Heavenly Father may not always reveal Himself as quickly as you would like. But rest assured: God is here, and He intends to use you in wonderful, unexpected ways. He desires to lead you along a path of His choosing. Your challenge is to watch, to listen, to learn . . . and to follow.

Peace and Prayer

Be cheerful no matter what; pray all the time; thank God no matter what happens. This is the way God wants you who belong to Christ Jesus to live.

1 THESSALONIANS 5:16-18 MSG

Do you seek a more peaceful life? Then you must lead a prayerful life. Do you have questions that you simply can't answer? Ask for the guidance of your Father in heaven. Do you sincerely seek the gift of everlasting love and eternal life? Accept the grace of God's only begotten Son.

When you weave the habit of prayer into the very fabric of your day, you invite God to become a partner in every aspect of your life. When you consult God on an constant basis, you avail yourself of His wisdom, His strength, and His love. And, because God answers prayers according to His perfect timetable, your petitions to Him will transform your family, your world, and yourself.

Today, turn everything over to your Creator in prayer. Instead of worrying about your next decision, decide to let God lead the way. Don't limit your prayers to meals or to bedtime. Pray constantly about things great and small. God is listening, and He wants to hear from you. Now.

Real Prosperity

Serving God does make us very rich, if we are satisfied with what we have. We brought nothing into the world, so we can take nothing out. But, if we have food and clothes, we will be satisfied with that.

1 TIMOTHY 6:6-8 NCV

We live in an era of prosperity, a time when many of us have been richly blessed with an assortment of material possessions that our forebears could have scarcely imagined. As believers living in these prosperous times, we must be cautious: we must keep prosperity in perspective.

The world stresses the importance of material possessions; God does not. The world offers the promise of happiness through wealth and public acclaim; God offers the promise of peace through His Son. When in doubt, we must distrust the world and trust God. The world often makes promises that it cannot keep, but when God makes a promise, He keeps it, not just for a day or a year or a lifetime, for all eternity.

Our ultimate aim in life is not to be healthy, wealthy, prosperous, or problem free. Our ultimate aim in life is to bring glory to God.

ANNE GRAHAM LOTZ

Who Rules Your Heart?

Give to the Lord the glory due His name; bring an offering, and come into His courts.

PSALM 96:8 NKJV

Who rules your heart? Is it God, or is it something else? Do you give God your firstfruits or your last? Have you given Christ your heart, your soul, your talents, your time, and your testimony? Or are you giving Him little more than a few hours each Sunday morning?

In the book of Exodus, God warns that we should place no gods before Him. Yet all too often, we place our Lord in second, third, or fourth place as we worship the gods of pride, greed, power, or personal gratification. When we unwittingly place possessions or relationships above our love for the Creator, we must seek His forgiveness and repent from our disobedience.

Does God rule your heart? Make certain that the honest answer to this question is a resounding yes. In the life of every righteous believer, God comes first. And that's precisely the place that He deserves in your heart.

Rest and Recharge Your Batteries

Come unto me, all ye that labor and are heavy laden, and I will give you rest.

MATTHEW 11:28 KJV

Even the most inspired Christians can, from time to time, find themselves running on empty. The demands of daily life can drain us of our strength and rob us of the joy that is rightfully ours in Christ. When we find ourselves tired, discouraged, or worse, there is a source from which we can draw the power needed to recharge our spiritual batteries. That source is God.

God intends that His children lead joyous lives filled with abundance and peace. But sometimes, abundance and peace seem very far away. It is then that we must turn to God for renewal, and when we do, He will restore us.

God expects us to work hard, but He also intends for us to rest. When we fail to take the rest that we need, we do a disservice to ourselves and to our families.

Is your spiritual battery running low? Is your energy on the wane? Are your emotions frayed? If so, it's time to turn your thoughts and your prayers to God. And when you're finished, it's time to rest.

He Wants Your Attention

Let us lay aside every weight and the sin that so easily ensnares us, and run with endurance the race that lies before us, keeping our eyes on Jesus, the source and perfecter of our faith.

HEBREWS 12:1-2 HCSB

Is yours a life of moderation or accumulation? Are you more interested in the possessions you can acquire or in the person you can become? The answers to these questions will determine the direction of your day and, in time, the direction of your life.

Ours is a highly complicated society, a place where people and corporations vie for your attention, for your time, and for your dollars. Don't let them succeed in complicating your life! Keep your eyes focused instead upon God.

If your material possessions are somehow distancing you from God, discard them. If your outside interests leave you too little time for your family or your Creator, slow down the merry-go-round, or better yet, get off the merry-go-round completely. Remember: God wants your full attention, and He wants it today, so don't let anybody or anything get in His way.

He Preserves Us

He will wipe away every tear from their eyes. Death will exist no longer; grief, crying, and pain will exist no longer, because the previous things have passed away.

REVELATION 21:4 HCSB

Women of every generation have experienced adversity, and this generation is no different. But, today's women face challenges that previous generations could have scarcely imagined. Thankfully, although the world continues to change, God's love remains constant. And, He remains ready to comfort us and strengthen us whenever we turn to Him.

God's Word promises, "The Lord is near to all who call upon Him, to all who call upon Him in truth. He will fulfill the desire of those who fear Him; He also will hear their cry and save them. The Lord preserves all who love Him" (Psalm 145:18-20). This comforting passage reminds us that when we are troubled, we should call upon God, and in time, He will heal us. And until He does, we may be comforted in the knowledge that we never suffer alone.

As we focus on His love and Word, in time He will fill our void and loneliness, and He will heal our pain.

ANITA CORRINE DONIHUE

Focusing on His Blessings

Blessed is he whose help is the God of Jacob, whose hope is in the LORD his God, the Maker of heaven and earth, the sea, and everything in them—the LORD, who remains faithful forever.

PSALM 146:5-6 NIV

What is your focus today? Are you willing to focus your thoughts on the countless blessings that God has bestowed upon you? Before you answer that question, consider this: the direction of your thoughts will determine, to a surprising extent, the direction of your day and your life.

This day—and every day hereafter—is a chance to celebrate the life that God has given you. It's a chance to celebrate your relationships, your talents, and your opportunities. So focus your thoughts upon the gift of life—and upon the blessings that surround you.

You're a beautiful creation of God, a being of infinite importance. Give thanks for your gifts and share them. Never have the needs—or the opportunities for service—been greater.

Preoccupy my thoughts with your praise beginning today.

JONI EARECKSON TADA

Practical Christianity

But prove yourselves doers of the word, and not merely hearers who delude themselves.

JAMES 1:22 NASB

As Christians, we must do our best to ensure that our actions are accurate reflections of our beliefs. Our theology must be demonstrated, not only by our words but, more importantly, by our actions. In short, we should be practical believers, quick to act whenever we see an opportunity to serve God.

Are you the kind of practical Christian who is willing to dig in and do what needs to be done when it needs to be done? If so, congratulations: God acknowledges your service and blesses it. But if you find yourself more interested in the fine points of theology than in the needs of your neighbors, it's time to rearrange your priorities. God needs believers who are willing to roll up their sleeves and go to work for Him. Count yourself among that number. Theology is a good thing unless it interferes with God's work. And it's up to you to make certain that your theology doesn't.

New Beginnings

Do not remember the former things, nor consider the things of old. Behold, I will do a new thing.

ISAIAH 43:18-19 NKJV

Each new day offers countless opportunities to serve God, to seek His will, and to obey His teachings. But each day also offers countless opportunities to stray from God's commandments and to wander far from His path.

Sometimes, we wander aimlessly in a wilderness of our own making, but God has better plans of us. And, whenever we ask Him to renew our strength and guide our steps, He does so.

Consider this day a new beginning. Consider it a fresh start, a renewed opportunity to serve your Creator with willing hands and a loving heart. Ask God to renew your sense of purpose as He guides your steps. Today is a glorious opportunity to serve God. Seize that opportunity while you can; tomorrow may indeed be too late.

Prayer is the way to open ourselves to God, and the way in which He shows us our unstable hearts and begins to strengthen them.

ST. TERESA OF AVILA

His Love Endures

But the love of the Lord remains forever with those who fear him. His salvation extends to the children's children of those who are faithful to his covenant, of those who obey his commandments!

PSALM 103:17-18 NLT

Are you anxious about situations that you cannot control? Take your anxieties to God. Are you troubled by changes that threaten to disrupt your life? Take your troubles to Him. Does your corner of the world seem to be shaking beneath your feet? Seek protection from the One who cannot be moved.

The same God who created the universe will protect you if you ask Him . . . so ask Him . . . and then serve Him with willing hands and a trusting heart. Rest assured that the world may change moment by moment, but God's love—a love that is unfathomable and unchanging—endures forever.

We do not love each other without changing each other. We do not observe the world around us without in some way changing it, and being changed ourselves.

MADELEINE L'ENGLE

When Your Courage Is Tested

But Moses said to the people, "Do not fear! Stand by and see the salvation of the LORD."

EXODUS 14:13 NASB

Jesus has won the victory, so all Christians should live courageously, including you. If you have been touched by the transforming hand of God's Son, then you have every reason to be confident about your future here on earth and your future in heaven. But even if you are a faithful believer, you may find yourself discouraged by the inevitable disappointments and tragedies that are the inevitable price of life here on earth.

If your courage is being tested today, lean upon God's promises. Trust His Son. Remember that God is always near and that He is your protector and your deliverer. When you are worried, anxious, or afraid, call upon Him and accept the touch of His comforting hand. Remember that God rules both mountaintops and valleys—with limitless wisdom and love—now and forever.

What is courage? It is the ability to be strong in trust, in conviction, in obedience. To be courageous is to step out in faith—to trust and obey, no matter what.

KAY ARTHUR

When People Misbehave

Don't worry because of evildoers, and don't envy the wicked.

PROVERBS 24:19 HCSB

Sometimes, people can be discourteous and cruel. Sometimes people can be unfair, unkind, and unappreciative. Sometimes people get angry and frustrated. So what's a Christian to do? God's answer is straightforward: forgive, forget, and move on. In Luke 6:37, Jesus instructs, "Do not judge, and you will not be judged. Do not condemn, and you will not be condemned. Forgive, and you will be forgiven" (HCSB).

Today and every day, make sure that you're quick to forgive others for their shortcomings. And when other people misbehave (as they most certainly will from time to time), don't pay too much attention. Just forgive those people as quickly as you can, and try to move on . . . as quickly as you can.

A keen sense of humor helps us to overlook the unbecoming, understand the unconventional, tolerate the unpleasant, overcome the unexpected, and outlast the unbearable.

BILLY GRAHAM

Speaking Words of Encouragement and Hope

Good people's words will help many others.

PROVERBS 10:21 NCV

The words that we speak have the power to do great good or great harm. If we speak words of encouragement and hope, we can lift others up. And that's exactly what God commands us to do!

Sometimes, when we feel uplifted and secure, it is easy to speak kind words. Other times, when we are discouraged or tired, we can scarcely summon the energy to uplift ourselves, much less anyone else. God intends that we speak words of kindness, wisdom, and truth, no matter our circumstances, no matter our emotions. When we do, we share a priceless gift with the world, and we give glory to the One who gave His life for us. As believers, we must do no less.

We do have the ability to encourage or discourage each other with the words we say. In order to maintain a positive mood, our hearts must be in good condition.

ANNIE CHAPMAN

Faith and Wholeness

Now the just shall live by faith.

HEBREWS 10:38 NKJV

A suffering woman sought healing in an unusual way: she simply touched the hem of Jesus' garment. When she did, Jesus turned and said, "Daughter, be of good comfort; thy faith hath made thee whole" (Matthew 9:22 KJV). We, too, can be made whole when we place our faith completely and unwaveringly in the person of Jesus Christ.

When you place your faith, your trust, indeed your life in the hands of Christ Jesus, you'll be amazed at the marvelous things He can do with you and through you. So strengthen your faith through praise, through worship, through Bible study, and through prayer. Then, trust God's plans. Your Heavenly Father is standing at the door of your heart. If you reach out to Him in faith, He will give you peace and heal your broken spirit. Be content to touch even the smallest fragment of the Master's garment, and He will make you whole.

Faith does not concern itself with the entire journey. One step is enough.

MRS. CHARLES E. COWMAN

Forgive Everybody!

Be kind to one another, tender-hearted, forgiving each other, just as God in Christ also has forgiven you.

EPHESIANS 4:32 NASB

From time to time, all of us fall prey to a powerful yet subtle temptation: the temptation to judge others. But the Bible teaches us to refrain from such behavior. The warning is unmistakably clear: "Judge not, and ye shall not be judged." In other words, we must refrain from being judgmental . . . or else.

Thankfully, the Bible promises that God has forgiven us (whew!). Now it's our turn to forgive others. So, let us refrain from the temptation to judging our family members, our friends, and our loved ones. And let us refrain from judging people we don't know very well (or people we don't know at all). Instead, let us forgive everybody (including ourselves!) in the same way that God forgives: completely.

Forgiveness enables you to bury your grudge in icy earth. To put the past behind you. To flush resentment away by being the first to forgive. Forgiveness fashions your future. It is a brave and brash thing to do.

BARBARA JOHNSON

He Taught Us to Be Generous

I have shown you in every way, by laboring like this, that you must support the weak. And remember the words of the Lord Jesus, that He said, "It is more blessed to give than to receive."

ACTS 20:35 NKJV

The thread of generosity is woven—completely and inextricably—into the very fabric of Christ's teachings. As He sent His disciples out to heal the sick and spread God's message of salvation, Jesus offered this guiding principle: Freely you have received, freely give (Matthew 10:8 NIV). The principle still applies. If we are to be disciples of Christ, we must give freely of our time, our possessions, and our love.

Lisa Whelchel observed, "The Lord has abundantly blessed me all of my life. I'm not trying to pay Him back for all of His wonderful gifts; I just realize that He gave them to me to give away." All of us have been blessed, and all of us are called to share those blessings without reservation.

Today, make this pledge and keep it: Be a cheerful, generous, courageous giver. The world needs your help, and you need the spiritual rewards that will be yours when you share your possessions, your talents, and your time.

His Glorious World

*The heavens declare the glory of God, and the sky proclaims
the work of His hands.*

PSALM 19:1 HCSB

Each morning, the sun rises upon a glorious world
that is a physical manifestation of God's infinite
power and His infinite love. And yet we're sometimes
too busy to notice.

We live in a society filled with more distractions
than we can possibly count and more obligations than
we can possibly meet. Is it any wonder, then, that we
often overlook God's handiwork as we rush from place
to place, giving scarcely a single thought to the beauty
that surrounds us?

Today, take time to really observe the world around
you. Take time to offer a pray of thanks for the sky
above and the beauty that lies beneath it. And take time
to ponder the miracle of God's creation. The time you
spend celebrating God's wonderful world is always time
well spent.

Out of him we have all come, in him we are all enfolded
and towards him we are all journeying.

JULIANA OF NORWICH

His Watchful Eye

O Lord, you have examined my heart and know everything about me. You know when I sit down or stand up. You know my every thought when far away. You chart the path ahead of me and tell me where to stop and rest.

PSALM 139:1-3 NLT

The heart of God is all-knowing. Even when nobody else is watching, God is watching. Even when we believe that the consequences of our actions will be known only to ourselves, our Creator sees our actions, and He responds accordingly. Ours is a God who, in His own time and in His own way, rewards righteousness and punishes sin. It's as simple as that.

Nothing that we say or do escapes the watchful eye of our Lord. God understands that we are not perfect, and He understands that we will inevitably make mistakes, but He wants us to live according to His rules, not our own. And when we don't, He does not protect us from the natural consequences of our mistakes.

The next time that you're tempted to say something that you shouldn't say or do something that you shouldn't do, remember that you can't keep secrets from the all-knowing heart of God. So don't even try!

When Grief Visits

God, who comforts the downcast, comforted us . . . .

2 CORINTHIANS 7:6 NIV

Grief visits all of us who live long and love deeply. When we lose a loved one, or when we experience any other profound loss, darkness overwhelms us for a while, and it seems as if we cannot summon the strength to face another day—but, with God's help, we can.

Thankfully, God promises that He is "close to the brokenhearted" (Psalm 34:18 NIV). In times of intense sadness, we can turn to Him, and we can turn to close friends and family. When we do, we can be comforted . . . and in time we will be healed.

Concentration camp survivor Corrie ten Boom noted, "There is no pit so deep that God's love is not deeper still." Let us remember those words and live by them . . . especially when the days seem dark.

Mercy is not the ability to no longer feel the pain and heartache of living in this world. Mercy is knowing that I am being held through the pain by my Father.

ANGELA THOMAS

The Crucial Question

Then Jesus said to his disciples, "If anyone would come after me, he must deny himself and take up his cross and follow me. For whoever wants to save his life will lose it, but whoever loses his life for me will find it."

MATTHEW 16:24-25 NIV

The 19th-century writer Hannah Whitall Smith observed, "The crucial question for each of us is this: What do you think of Jesus, and do you yet have a personal acquaintance with Him?" Indeed, the answer to that question determines the quality, the course, and the direction of our lives today and for all eternity.

The old familiar hymn begins, "What a friend we have in Jesus . . . ." No truer words were ever penned. Jesus is the sovereign friend and ultimate Savior of mankind. Christ showed enduring love for His believers by willingly sacrificing His own life so that we might have eternal life. Now, it is our turn to become His friend.

Let us love our Savior, praise Him, and share His message of salvation with our neighbors and with the world. When we do, we demonstrate that our acquaintance with the Master is not a passing fancy; it is, instead, the cornerstone and the touchstone of our lives.

Life Triumphant

Shout triumphantly to the Lord, all the earth. Serve the
Lord with gladness; come before Him with joyful songs.
PSALM 100:1-2 HCSB

Are you living the triumphant life that God
has promised? Or are you, instead, a spiritual
shrinking violet? As you ponder that question, consider
this: God does not intend that you live a life that is
commonplace or mediocre. And He doesn't want you
to hide your light "under a basket." Instead, He wants
you to "Let your light so shine before men, that they
may see your good works and glorify your Father in
heaven" (Matthew 5:16 NKJV). In short, God wants
you to live a triumphant life so that others might know
precisely what it means to be a believer.

The Christian life should be a triumphal celebration,
a daily exercise in thanksgiving and praise. Join that
celebration today. And while you're at it, make sure that
you let others know that you've joined.

The measure of a man is not what he does on Sunday,
but rather who he is Monday through Saturday.

ANONYMOUS

When We Worship Money

No servant can serve two masters. The servant will hate one master and love the other, or will follow one master and refuse to follow the other. You cannot serve both God and worldly riches.

Luke 16:13 NCV

Your money can be used as a blessing to yourself and to others, but beware: You live in a society that places far too much importance on money and the things that money can buy. God does not. God cares about people, not possessions, and so must you.

Money, in and of itself, is not evil; worshipping money is. So today, as you prioritize matters of importance for you and yours, remember that God is almighty, but the dollar is not.

If we worship God, we are blessed. But if we worship "the almighty dollar," we are inevitably punished because of our misplaced priorities—and our punishment inevitably comes sooner rather than later.

Have you prayed about your resources lately? Find out how God wants you to use your time and your money. No matter what it costs, forsake all that is not of God.

Kay Arthur

Perspective Now

Teach me Your way, O LORD; I will walk in Your truth.
PSALM 86:11 NASB

For most of us, life is busy and complicated. Amid the rush and crush of the daily grind, it is easy to lose perspective . . . easy, but wrong. When our world seems to be spinning out of control, we must simply seek to regain perspective by slowing ourselves down and then turning our thoughts and prayers toward God.

Do you carve out quiet moments each day to offer thanksgiving and praise to your Creator? You should. During these moments of stillness, you will often sense the love and wisdom of our Lord.

The familiar words of Psalm 46:10 remind us to "Be still, and know that I am God" (NKJV). When we do so, we encounter the awesome presence of our loving Heavenly Father, and we are blessed beyond words. But, when we ignore the presence of our Creator, we rob ourselves of His perspective, His peace, and His joy.

Today and every day, make time to be still before God. When you do, you can face the day's complications with the wisdom and power that only He can provide.

Prayer Changes Things and You

And everything—whatever you ask in prayer, believing—
you will receive.

MATTHEW 21:22 HCSB

Is prayer an integral part of your daily life or is it a hit-or-miss habit? Do you "pray without ceasing," or is your prayer life an afterthought? As you consider the role that prayer currently plays in your life—and the role that you think it should play—remember that the quality of your spiritual life is inevitably related to the quality of your prayer life.

Prayer changes things and it changes you. So today, instead of turning things over in your mind, turn them over to God in prayer. Instead of worrying about your next decision, pray about it. Don't limit your prayers to meals or to bedtime. Pray often about things great and small. God is listening, and He wants to hear from you. Now.

I pray God will open the eyes of women everywhere to the Liberator who has given His life to set them free from spiritual, social, and psychological bondage.

ANNE GRAHAM LOTZ

Your Next Move

It is better to take refuge in the Lord than to trust in man.

PSALM 118:8 HCSB

oes God have a plan for your life? Of course He does! Every day of your life, He is trying to lead you along a path of His choosing . . . but He won't force you to follow. God has given you free will, the opportunity to make decisions for yourself. The choices are yours: either you will choose to obey His Word and seek His will, or you will choose to follow a different path.

Today, as you carve out a few quiet moments to commune with your Heavenly Father, ask Him to renew your sense of purpose. God's plans for you may be far bigger than you imagine, but He may be waiting for you to make the next move—so today, make that move prayerfully, faithfully, and expectantly. And after you've made your move, trust God to make His.

Your job may be and ideally should be part of your mission, but a mission is always larger than a job. Jobs can change—and probably will.

LAURIE BETH JONES

Disciplining Yourself

Therefore, get your minds ready for action, being self-disciplined, and set your hope completely on the grace to be brought to you at the revelation of Jesus Christ. As obedient children, do not be conformed to the desires of your former ignorance but, as the One who called you is holy, you also are to be holy in all your conduct.

1 PETER 1:13-15 HCSB

God's Word is clear: as believers, we are called to lead lives of discipline, diligence, moderation, and maturity. But the world often tempts us to do otherwise. Everywhere we turn, or so it seems, we are faced with powerful temptations to behave in undisciplined, ungodly ways—but God has far better plans for our days and for our lives.

God's Word instructs us to be disciplined in our thoughts and our actions; God's Word warns us against the dangers of impulsive behavior. God's Word teaches us that diligence is rewarded and laziness is not.

Do you seek to reap the rewards that God offers those who lead disciplined lives? If so, then you must learn to discipline yourself . . . before God does.

The Journey Toward Spiritual Maturity

For this reason also, since the day we heard this, we haven't stopped praying for you. We are asking that you may be filled with the knowledge of His will in all wisdom and spiritual understanding.

COLOSSIANS 1:9 HCSB

The journey toward spiritual maturity lasts a lifetime: As Christians, we can and should continue to grow in the love and the knowledge of our Savior as long as we live. Norman Vincent Peale had simple advice for believers of all ages: "Ask the God who made you to keep remaking you." That advice, of course, is perfectly sound, but too often ignored.

When we cease to grow, either emotionally or spiritually, we do ourselves and our families a profound disservice. But, if we study God's Word, if we obey His commandments, and if we live in the center of His will, we will not be "stagnant" believers; we will, instead, be growing Christians . . . and that's exactly what God wants for our lives.

In those quiet moments when we open our hearts to God, the Creator who made us keeps remaking us. He gives us direction, perspective, wisdom, and courage. And, the appropriate moment to accept His spiritual gifts is always this one.

Thank Him Now

Our prayers for you are always spilling over into thanksgivings. We can't quit thanking God our Father and Jesus our Messiah for you!

Colossians 1:3 MSG

Sometimes, life-here-on-earth can be complicated, demanding, and frustrating. When the demands of life leave us rushing from place to place with scarcely a moment to spare, we may fail to pause and thank our Creator for the countless blessings He bestows upon us. But, whenever we neglect to give proper thanks to the Giver of all things good, we suffer because of our misplaced priorities.

As believers who have been saved by a risen Christ, we are blessed beyond human comprehension. We who have been given so much should make thanksgiving a habit, a regular part of our daily routines. Of course, God's gifts are too numerous to count, but we should attempt to count them nonetheless. We owe our Heavenly Father everything, including our eternal praise . . . starting right now.

If you pause to think—you'll have cause to thank!

Anonymous

Seeking His Blessings

Commit everything you do to the Lord. Trust him, and he will help you.

PSALM 37:5 NLT

When our dreams come true and our plans prove successful, we find it easy to thank our Creator and easy to trust His divine providence. But in times of sorrow or hardship, we may find ourselves questioning God's plans for our lives.

On occasion, you will confront circumstances that trouble you to the very core of your soul. It is during these difficult days that you must find the wisdom and the courage to trust your Heavenly Father despite your circumstances.

Are you a woman who seeks God's blessings for yourself and your family? Then trust Him. Trust Him with your relationships. Trust Him with your priorities. Follow His commandments and pray for His guidance. Trust your Heavenly Father day by day, moment by moment—in good times and in trying times. Then, wait patiently for God's revelations . . . and prepare yourself for the abundance and peace that will most certainly be yours when you do.

Beyond the World's Wisdom

For the wisdom of this world is foolishness in God's sight.
1 CORINTHIANS 3:19 NIV

The world has its own brand of wisdom, a brand of wisdom that is often wrong and sometimes dangerous. God, on the other hand, has a different brand of wisdom, a wisdom that will never lead you astray. Where will you place your trust today? Will you trust in the wisdom of fallible men and women, or will you place your faith in God's perfect wisdom? The answer to this question will determine the direction of your day and the quality of your decisions.

Are you tired? Discouraged? Fearful? Be comforted and trust God. Are you worried or anxious? Be confident in God's power. Are you confused? Listen to the quiet voice of your Heavenly Father—He is not a God of confusion. Talk with Him; listen to Him; trust Him. His wisdom, unlike the "wisdom" of the world, will never let you down.

Knowledge can be learned, but wisdom must be earned. Wisdom is knowledge . . . lived.

SHEILA WALSH

Taking Your Worries to God

Give your worries to the Lord, and he will take care of you. He will never let good people down.

PSALM 55:22 NCV

Because life is sometimes difficult, and because we have understandable fears about the uncertainty of the future, we worry. At times, we may find ourselves fretting over the countless details of everyday life. We may worry about our relationships, our finances, our health, or any number of potential problems, some large and some small.

If you're a "worrier" by nature, it's probably time to rethink the way that you think! Perhaps you've formed the unfortunate habit of focusing too intently on negative aspects of life while spending too little time counting your blessings. If so, take your worries to God . . . and leave them there. When you do, you'll learn to worry a little less and to trust God a little more—and that's as it should be because God is trustworthy, you are protected, and your future can be intensely bright.

Worship and worry cannot live in the same heart; they are mutually exclusive.

RUTH BELL GRAHAM

Expecting God's Blessings

My cup runs over. Surely goodness and mercy shall follow me all the days of my life; and I will dwell in the house of the Lord forever.

PSALM 23:5-6 NKJV

As you look at the landscape of your life, do you see opportunities, possibilities, and blessings, or do you focus, instead, upon the more negative scenery? Do you spend more time counting your blessings or your misfortunes? If you've acquired the unfortunate habit of focusing too intently upon the negative aspects of life, then your spiritual vision is in need of correction.

Today is yet another gift from God, and it presents yet another opportunity to thank Him for His gifts . . . or not. And if you're wise, you'll give thanks early and often.

The way that you choose to view the scenery around you will have a profound impact on the quality, the tone, and the direction of your life. The more you focus on the beauty that surrounds you, the more beautiful your own life becomes.

Developing a positive attitude means working continually to find what is uplifting and encouraging.

BARBARA JOHNSON

His Healing Touch

"I will give peace, real peace, to those far and near, and I will heal them," says the Lord.

ISAIAH 57:19 NCV

Are you concerned about your spiritual, physical, or emotional health? If so, there is a timeless source of comfort and assurance that is as near as your next breath. That source of comfort, of course, is God.

God is concerned about every aspect of your life, including your health. And, when you face concerns of any sort—including health-related challenges—God is with you. So trust your medical doctor to do his or her part, and turn to your family and friends for moral, physical, and spiritual support. But don't be afraid to place your ultimate trust in your benevolent Heavenly Father. His healing touch, like His love, endures forever.

Jesus Christ is the One by whom, for whom, through whom everything was made. Therefore, He knows what's wrong in your life and how to fix it.

ANNE GRAHAM LOTZ

His Abundance

I have come that they may have life, and that they may have it more abundantly.

JOHN 10:10 NKJV

The Bible gives us hope—as Christians we can enjoy lives filled with abundance.

But what, exactly, did Jesus mean when, in John 10:10, He promised "life . . . more abundantly"? Was He referring to material possessions or financial wealth? Hardly. Jesus offers a different kind of abundance: a spiritual richness that extends beyond the temporal boundaries of this world.

Is material abundance part of God's plan for our lives? Perhaps. But in every circumstance of life, during times of wealth or times of want, God will provide us what we need if we trust Him (Matthew 6). May we, as believers, claim the riches of Christ Jesus every day that we live, and may we share His blessings with all who cross our path.

Jesus intended for us to be overwhelmed by the blessings of regular days. He said it was the reason he had come: "I am come that they might have life, and that they might have it more abundantly."

GLORIA GAITHER

When Calamity Strikes

Why am I so depressed? Why this turmoil within me? Put your hope in God, for I will still praise Him, my Savior and my God.

PSALM 42:11 HCSB

When calamity strikes anywhere in the world, we may be confronted with real-time images, images that breed anxiety. And as we stare transfixed at our television screens, we may fall prey to fear, discouragement, worry, or all three. But our Father in heaven has other plans. God has promised that we may lead lives of abundance, not anxiety. In fact, His Word instructs us to "be anxious for nothing" (Philippians 4:6). But how can we put our fears to rest? By taking those fears to God and leaving them there.

As you face the challenges of daily life, you may find yourself becoming anxious. If so, turn every one of your concerns over to your Heavenly Father. The same God who created the universe will comfort you if you ask Him . . . so ask Him and trust Him. And then watch in amazement as your anxieties melt into the warmth of His loving hands.

Born Again

Whatever is born of the flesh is flesh, and whatever is born of the Spirit is spirit.

JOHN 3:6 HCSB

Why did Christ die on the cross? Christ sacrificed His life so that we might be born again. This gift, freely given from God's only begotten Son, is the priceless possession of everyone who accepts Him as Lord and Savior.

God is waiting patiently for each of us to accept the gift of eternal life. Let us claim Christ's gift today. Let us walk with the Savior, let us love Him, let us praise Him, and let us share His message of salvation with all those who cross our paths.

The comforting words of Ephesians 2:8 make God's promise clear: "For by grace you have been saved through faith, and that not of yourselves; it is the gift of God" (NKJV). Thus, we are saved not because of our good deeds but because of our faith in Christ. May we, who have been given so much, praise our Savior for the gift of salvation, and may we share the joyous news of our Master's limitless love with our families, with our friends, and with the world.

Choosing to Walk in His Footsteps

The thing you should want most is God's kingdom and doing what God wants. Then all these other things you need will be given to you.

Matthew 6:33 NCV

Because we are creatures of free will, we make choices—lots of them. When we make choices that are pleasing to our Heavenly Father, we are blessed. When we make choices that cause us to walk in the footsteps of God's Son, we enjoy the abundance that Christ has promised to those who follow Him. But when make choices that are displeasing to God, we sow seeds that have the potential to bring forth a bitter harvest.

Today, as you encounter the challenges of everyday living, you will make hundreds of choices. Choose wisely. Make your thoughts and your actions pleasing to God. And remember: every choice that is displeasing to Him is the wrong choice—no exceptions.

Freedom is not the right to do what we want but the power to do what we ought.

Corrie ten Boom

Courtesy Matters

Be hospitable to one another without grumbling.

1 PETER 4:9 NKJV

D id Christ instruct us in matters of etiquette and courtesy? Of course He did. Christ's instructions are clear: "In everything, therefore, treat people the same way you want them to treat you, for this is the Law and the Prophets" (Matthew 7:12 NASB). Jesus did not say, "In some things, treat people as you wish to be treated." And, He did not say, "From time to time, treat others with kindness." Christ said that we should treat others as we wish to be treated in every aspect of our daily lives. This, of course, is a tall order indeed, but as Christians, we are commanded to do our best.

Today, be a little kinder than necessary to family members, friends, and total strangers. And, as you consider all the things that Christ has done in your life, honor Him with your words and with your deeds. He expects no less, and He deserves no less.

Reach out and care for someone who needs the touch of hospitality. The time you spend caring today will be a love gift that will blossom into the fresh joy of God's Spirit in the future.

EMILIE BARNES

Your Great Expectations

When dreams come true, there is life and joy.

PROVERBS 13:12 NLT

Do you expect your future to be bright? Are you willing to dream king-sized dreams . . . and are you willing to work diligently to make those dreams happen? Hopefully so—after all, God promises that we can do "all things" through Him. Yet most of us, even the most devout among us, live far below our potential. We take half measures; we dream small dreams; we waste precious time and energy on the distractions of the world. But God has other plans for us.

Our Creator intends that we live faithfully, hopefully, courageously, and abundantly. He knows that we are capable of so much more; and He wants us to do the things we're capable of doing; and He wants us to begin doing those things today.

God created us with an overwhelming desire to soar. He designed us to be tremendously productive and "to mount up with wings like eagles," realistically dreaming of what He can do with our potential.

CAROL KENT

The Adversary Prowls

Be careful! Watch out for attacks from the Devil, your great enemy. He prowls around like a roaring lion, looking for some victim to devour. Take a firm stand against him, and be strong in your faith.

1 PETER 5:8-9 NLT

This world is God's creation, and it contains the wonderful fruits of His handiwork. But, it also contains countless opportunities to stray from God's will. Temptations are everywhere, and the devil, it seems, never takes a day off. Our task, as believers, is to turn away from temptation and to place our lives squarely in the center of God's will.

In a letter to believers, Peter offers a stern warning: "Your adversary, the devil, prowls around like a roaring lion, seeking someone to devour" (1 Peter 5:8 NASB). What was true in New Testament times is equally true in our own. Satan tempts his prey and then devours them. As believing Christians, we must beware. And, if we seek righteousness in our own lives, we must earnestly wrap ourselves in the protection of God's Holy Word. When we do, we are secure.

Fellowship and Hope

I want their hearts to be encouraged and joined together in love, so that they may have all the riches of assured understanding, and have the knowledge of God's mystery—Christ.

COLOSSIANS 2:2 HCSB

Every believer—including you—needs to be part of a community of faith. Your association with fellow Christians should be uplifting, enlightening, encouraging, and consistent.

Are you an active member of your fellowship? Are you a builder of bridges inside the four walls of your church and outside it? Do you contribute to God's glory by contributing your time and your talents to a close-knit band of hope-filled believers? Hopefully so. The fellowship of believers is intended to be a powerful tool for spreading God's Good News and uplifting His children. And God intends for you to be a fully contributing member of that fellowship. Your intentions should be the same.

Christians are like coals of a fire. Together they glow—apart they grow cold.

ANONYMOUS

Talking About Forgiveness

The one who walks with the wise will become wise . . . .

PROVERBS 13:20 HCSB

If you simply can't find it in your heart to forgive someone, perhaps it's time to talk things over with a person you trust. Perhaps that person is a friend or family member. Or perhaps that person is your pastor or your pastoral counselor.

Sometimes, it takes other people to help us see the obvious: forgiveness is a gift that we give to ourselves. It is only when we forgive others that we gain peace for ourselves. It is only when we empty our hearts of bitterness that we can fill our hearts with joy. It is only when we no longer wish unhappiness for others that we can find lasting happiness for ourselves.

If your heart is burdened with anger or regret, talk about it but don't obsess about it. Your goal should be simple: to forgive and move on. Why? Because the person who hurt you may need your forgiveness, but the one who benefits most from your forgiveness is you.

God expects us to forgive others as He has forgiven us; we are to follow His example by having a forgiving heart.

VONETTE BRIGHT

God's Comfort

Praise be to the God and Father of our Lord Jesus Christ. God is the Father who is full of mercy and all comfort. He comforts us every time we have trouble, so when others have trouble, we can comfort them with the same comfort God gives us.

2 CORINTHIANS 1:3-4 NCV

We live in a world that is, at times, a frightening place. We live in a world that is, at times, a discouraging place. We live in a world where life-changing losses can be so painful and so profound that it seems we will never recover. But with God's help, and with the help of encouraging family members and friends, we can recover.

During the darker days of life, we are wise to remember that God is with us always and that He offers us comfort, assurance, and peace—our task, of course, is to accept these gifts.

When we trust in God's promises, the world becomes a less frightening place. With God's comfort and His love in our hearts, we can tackle our problems with courage, determination, and faith.

A Gift Beyond Comprehension

Therefore, since we are receiving a kingdom that cannot be shaken, let us hold on to grace. By it, we may serve God acceptably, with reverence and awe.

HEBREWS 12:28 HCSB

The grace of God overflows from His heart. And if we open our hearts to Him, we receive His grace, and we are blessed with joy, abundance, peace, and eternal life.

The familiar words of Ephesians 2:8 make God's promise perfectly clear: "For by grace you have been saved through faith, and that not of yourselves; it is the gift of God" (NKJV). In other words, we are saved, not by our actions, but by God's mercy. We are saved, not because of our good deeds, but because of our faith in Christ.

God's grace is the ultimate gift, a gift beyond comprehension and beyond compare. And because it is the ultimate gift, we owe God the ultimate in thanksgiving.

God's grace is indeed a gift from the heart—God's heart. And as believers, we must accept God's precious gift thankfully, humbly, and, immediately—today is never too soon because tomorrow may be too late.

God's Promises

Let's keep a firm grip on the promises that keep us going.
He always keeps his word.

HEBREWS 10:23 MSG

God's Word contains promises upon which we, as Christians, can and must depend. The Bible is a priceless gift, a tool that God intends for us to use in every aspect of our lives. Too many Christians, however, keep their spiritual tool kits tightly closed and out of sight.

Are you tired? Discouraged? Fearful? Be comforted and trust the promises that God has made to you. Are you worried or anxious? Be confident in God's power. He will never desert you. Do you see a difficult future ahead? Be courageous and call upon God. He will protect you and then use you according to His purposes. Are you confused? Listen to the quiet voice of your Heavenly Father. He is not a God of confusion. Talk with Him; listen to Him; trust Him, and trust His promises. He is steadfast, and He is your Protector . . . forever.

God's Sufficiency

My grace is sufficient for you, for My strength is made perfect in weakness.

2 CORINTHIANS 12:9 NKJV

O f this you can be sure: the loving heart of God is sufficient to meet your needs. Whatever dangers you may face, whatever heartbreaks you must endure, God is with you, and He stands ready to comfort you and to heal you.

The Psalmist writes, "Weeping may endure for a night, but joy comes in the morning" (Psalm 30:5 NKJV). But when we are suffering, the morning may seem very far away. It is not. God promises that He is "near to those who have a broken heart" (Psalm 34:18 NKJV. In times of intense sadness, we must turn to Him, and we must encourage our friends and family members to do likewise.

If you are experiencing the intense pain of a recent loss, or if you are still mourning a loss from long ago, perhaps you are now ready to begin the next stage of your journey with God. If so, be mindful of this fact: the loving heart of God is sufficient to meet any challenge, including yours. Trust the sufficient heart of God.

The Self-fulfilling Prophecy

But as for me, I will hope continually, and will praise You yet more and more.

PSALM 71:14 NASB

The self-fulfilling prophecy is alive, well, and living at your house. If you trust God and have faith for the future, your optimistic beliefs will give you direction and motivation. That's one reason that you should never lose hope, but certainly not the only reason. The primary reason that you, as a believer, should never lose hope, is because of God's unfailing promises.

Make no mistake about it: thoughts are powerful things: your thoughts have the power to lift you up or to hold you down. When you acquire the habit of hopeful thinking, you will have acquired a powerful tool for improving your life. So if you find yourself falling into the spiritual traps of worry and discouragement, seek the healing touch of Jesus and the encouraging words of fellow Christians. And if you fall into the terrible habit of negative thinking, think again. After all, God's Word teaches us that Christ can overcome every difficulty (John 16:33). And when God makes a promise, He keeps it.

Kindness Now

God has chosen you and made you his holy people. He loves you. So always do these things: Show mercy to others, be kind, humble, gentle, and patient.

COLOSSIANS 3:12 NCV

Christ showed His love for us by willingly sacrificing His own life so that we might have eternal life: "But God demonstrates his own love for us in this: While we were still sinners, Christ died for us" (Romans 5:8 NIV). We, as Christ's followers, are challenged to share His love with kind words on our lips and praise in our hearts.

Just as Christ has been—and will always be—the ultimate friend to His flock, so should we be Christlike in the kindness and generosity that we show toward others, especially those who are most in need.

When we walk each day with Jesus—and obey the commandments found in God's Holy Word—we become worthy ambassadors for Christ. When we share the love of Christ, we share a priceless gift with the world. As His servants, we must do no less.

Do You Believe in Miracles?

With God's power working in us, God can do much, much more than anything we can ask or imagine.

EPHESIANS 3:20 NCV

Do you believe in an all-powerful God who can do miraculous things in you and through you? You should. But perhaps, as you have faced the inevitable struggles of life you have—without realizing it—placed limitations on God. To do so is a profound mistake. God's power has no such limitations, and He can work mighty miracles in your own life if you let Him.

Do you lack a firm faith in God's power to perform miracles for you and your loved ones? If so, you are attempting to place limitations on a God who has none. Instead of doubting your Heavenly Father, you must place yourself in His hands. Instead of doubting God's power, you must trust it. Expect Him to work miracles, and be watchful. With God, absolutely nothing is impossible, including an amazing assortment of miracles that He stands ready, willing, and perfectly able to perform for you and yours.

God specializes in things thought impossible.

CATHERINE MARSHALL

Taking Up His Cross

Then He said to them all, "If anyone desires to come after Me, let him deny himself, and take up his cross daily, and follow Me. For whoever desires to save his life will lose it, but whoever loses his life for My sake will save it."

LUKE 9:23-24 NKJV

When Jesus addressed His disciples, He warned that each one must, "take up his cross and follow me." The disciples must have known exactly what the Master meant. In Jesus' day, prisoners were forced to carry their own crosses to the location where they would be put to death. Thus, Christ's message was clear: in order to follow Him, Christ's disciples must deny themselves and, instead, trust Him completely. Nothing has changed since then.

If we are to be dutiful disciples of the One from Galilee, we must trust Him and we must follow Him. Jesus never comes "next." He is always first. He shows us the path of life.

Do you seek to be a worthy disciple of Jesus? Then pick up His cross today and follow in His footsteps. When you do, you can walk with confidence: He will never lead you astray.

Our Hopes and His Peace

And as they thus spake, Jesus himself stood in the midst of them, and saith unto them, Peace be unto you.

LUKE 24:36 KJV

The beautiful words of John 14:27 give us hope: "Peace I leave with you, my peace I give unto you . . . ." Jesus offers us peace, not as the world gives, but as He alone gives. We, as believers, can accept His peace or ignore it.

When we accept the peace of Jesus Christ into our hearts, our lives are transformed. And then, because we possess the gift of peace, we can share that gift with fellow Christians, family members, friends, and associates. If, on the other hand, we choose to ignore the gift of peace—for whatever reason—we cannot share what we do not possess.

As every woman knows, peace can be a scarce commodity in a demanding, 21st-century world. How, then, can we find the peace that we so desperately desire? By turning our days and our lives over to God. Elisabeth Elliot writes, "If my life is surrendered to God, all is well. Let me not grab it back, as though it were in peril in His hand but would be safer in mine!" May we give our lives, our hopes, and our prayers to the Lord, and, by doing so, accept His will and His peace.

Your Potential

Have faith in the Lord your God, and you will stand strong. Have faith in his prophets, and you will succeed.
2 Chronicles 20:20 NCV

Do you expect your future to be bright? Are you willing to dream king-sized dreams . . . and are you willing to work diligently to make those dreams happen? Hopefully so—after all, God promises that we can do "all things" through Him. Yet most of us live far below our potential. We take half measures; we dream small dreams; we waste precious time and energy on the distractions of the world. God has other plans for us.

In her diary, Anne Frank wrote, "The good news is that you really don't know how great you can be, how much you can love, what you can accomplish, and what your potential is." These words apply to you. You possess great potential, potential that you must use or forfeit. And the time to fulfill that potential is now.

Christian women are often blocked form maximizing their potential because they do not understand the power of the Holy Spirit within them. A leader of women understands that every daughter of the King has been uniquely designed and equipped for a purpose.
Susan Hunt

Problem-solving

Teach me to do Your will, for You are my God. May Your gracious Spirit lead me on level ground.

PSALM 143:10 HCSB

Life is an exercise in problem-solving. The question is not whether we will encounter problems; the real question is how we will choose to address them. When it comes to solving the problems of everyday living, we often know precisely what needs to be done, but we may be slow in doing it—especially if what needs to be done is difficult or uncomfortable for us. So we put off till tomorrow what should be done today.

The words of Psalm 34 remind us that the Lord solves problems for "people who do what is right." And usually, doing "what is right" means doing the uncomfortable work of confronting our problems sooner rather than later. So with no further ado, let the problem-solving begin . . . now.

What a comfort to know that God is present there in your life, available to meet every situation with you, that you are never left to face any problem alone.

VONETTE BRIGHT

Right with God

The Good News shows how God makes people right with himself—that it begins and ends with faith. As the Scripture says, "But those who are right with God will live by trusting in him."

ROMANS 1:17 NCV

How do we live a life that is "right with God"? By accepting God's Son and obeying His commandments. Accepting Christ is a decision that we make one time; following in His footsteps requires thousands of decisions each day.

Whose steps will you follow today? Will you honor God as you strive to follow His Son? Or will you join the lockstep legion that seeks to discover happiness and fulfillment through worldly means? If you are righteous and wise, you will follow Christ. You will follow Him today and every day. You will seek to walk in His footsteps without reservation or doubt. When you do so, you will be "right with God" precisely because you are walking aright with His only begotten Son.

Christ has made my soul beautiful with the jewels of grace and virtue. I belong to Him whom the angels serve.

ST. AGNES

Simplicity

*Whoever becomes simple and elemental again, like this
child, will rank high in God's kingdom.*

MATTHEW 18:4 MSG

You live in a world where simplicity is in short
supply. Think for a moment about the complexity
of your everyday life and compare it to the lives of your
ancestors. Certainly, you are the beneficiary of many
technological innovations, but those innovations have a
price: in all likelihood, your world is highly complex.

Unless you take firm control of your time and your
life, you may be overwhelmed by an ever-increasing
tidal wave of complexity that threatens your happiness.
But your Heavenly Father understands the joy of living
simply, and so should you. So do yourself a favor: keep
your life as simple as possible. Simplicity is, indeed,
genius. By simplifying your life, you are destined to
improve it.

Some of my greatest spiritual moments have been
inspired by the unexpected and the simple.

MARILYN MEBERG

What We Become

For it is God who is working among you both the willing and the working for His good purpose.

PHILIPPIANS 2:13 HCSB

The old saying is both familiar and true: "What we are is God's gift to us; what we become is our gift to God." Each of us possesses special talents, gifted by God, that can be nurtured carefully or ignored totally. Our challenge, of course, is to use our abilities to the greatest extent possible and to use them in ways that honor our Savior.

Are you using your natural talents to make God's world a better place? If so, congratulations. But if you have gifts that you have not fully explored and developed, perhaps you need to have a chat with the One who gave you those gifts in the first place. Your talents are priceless treasures offered from your Heavenly Father. Use them. After all, an obvious way to say "thank you" to the Giver is to use the gifts He has given.

What we are is God's gift to us. What we become is our gift to God.

ANONYMOUS

Beyond Pessimism

But we are hoping for something we do not have yet, and we are waiting for it patiently.

ROMANS 8:25 NCV

When you decided to allow Christ to rule over your heart, you entitled yourself to share in His promise of spiritual abundance and eternal joy. Have you claimed that entitlement? Are you an upbeat believer? Are you a person whose hopes and dreams are alive and well? Hopefully so. But sometimes, when pessimism and doubt invade your thoughts, you won't feel like celebrating. Why? Because thoughts are extremely powerful things.

If you've allowed pessimism to creep into your mind and heart, you should spend more time thinking about your blessings and less time fretting about your hardships. Then, you should take time to thank the Giver of all things good for gifts that are, in truth, far too numerous to count.

Working in the vineyard, working all the day, never be discouraged, only watch and pray.

FANNY CROSBY

Overcoming the World

Whatever has been born of God conquers the world. This is the victory that has conquered the world: our faith.

1 John 5:4 HCSB

All of us face times of adversity. On occasion, we all must endure the disappointments and tragedies that befall believers and nonbelievers alike. The reassuring words of 1 John 5:4 remind us that when we accept God's grace, we overcome the passing hardships of this world by relying upon His strength, His love, and His promise of eternal life.

When we face the inevitable difficulties of life-here-on-earth, God stands ready to protect us. Our responsibility, of course, is to ask Him for protection. When we call upon Him in heartfelt prayer, He will answer—in His own time and according to His own plan—and He will heal us. And while we are waiting for God's plans to unfold and for His healing touch to restore us, we can be comforted in the knowledge that our Creator can overcome any obstacle, even if we cannot. Let us take God at His word, and let us trust Him.

Living Righteously

But now you must be holy in everything you do, just as God—who chose you to be his children—is holy. For he himself has said, "You must be holy because I am holy."

1 PETER 1:15-16 NLT

When we seek righteousness in our own lives—and when we seek the companionship of those who do likewise—we reap the spiritual rewards that God intends for us to enjoy. When we behave ourselves as godly men and women, we honor God. When we live righteously and according to God's commandments, He blesses us in ways that we cannot fully understand.

Today, as you fulfill your responsibilities, hold fast to that which is good, and associate yourself with believers who behave themselves in like fashion. When you do, your good works will serve as a powerful example for others and as a worthy offering to your Creator.

Do nothing that you would not like to be doing when Jesus comes. Go no place where you would not like to be found when He returns.

CORRIE TEN BOOM

Managing Change

The wise see danger ahead and avoid it, but fools keep going and get into trouble.

PROVERBS 27:12 NCV

There is no doubt. Your world is changing constantly. So today's question is this: How will you manage all those changes?" Will you do your best and trust God with the rest, or will you spend fruitless hours worrying about things you can't control, while doing precious little else? The answer to these simple questions will help determine the direction and quality of your life.

The best way to confront change is head-on . . . and with God by your side. The same God who created the universe will protect you if you ask Him, so ask Him—and then serve Him with willing hands and a trusting heart. When you do, you may rest assured that while the world changes moment by moment, God's love endures—unfathomable and unchanging—forever.

Conditions are always changing; therefore, I must not be dependent upon conditions. What matters supremely is my soul and my relationship to God.

CORRIE TEN BOOM

Trusting Your Conscience

Let us come near to God with a sincere heart and a sure faith, because we have been made free from a guilty conscience, and our bodies have been washed with pure water.

Hebrews 10:22 NCV

It has been said that character is what we are when nobody is watching. How true. When we do things that we know aren't right, we try to hide them from our families and friends. But even then, God is watching.

Few things in life torment us more than a guilty conscience. And, few things in life provide more contentment than the knowledge that we are obeying the conscience that God has placed in our hearts.

If you sincerely want to create the best possible life for yourself and your loved ones, never forsake your conscience. And remember this: when you walk with God, your character will take care of itself . . . and you won't need to look over your shoulder to see who, besides God, is watching.

Dealing with Difficult People

Bad temper is contagious—don't get infected.
PROVERBS 22:25 MSG

Face it: sometimes people can be difficult to deal with . . . very, very difficult. When other people are unkind to you, you may be tempted to strike back, either verbally or in some other way. Resist that temptation. Instead, remember that God corrects other people's behaviors in His own way, and He doesn't need your help (even if you're totally convinced that He does).

So when other people behave cruelly, foolishly, or impulsively—as they will from time to time—don't respond in kind. Instead, speak up for yourself as politely as you can, and walk away. Then, forgive everybody as quickly as you can and leave the rest up to God.

Discouraged people, if they must be discouraged, ought, at least, to keep their discouragements to themselves, hidden away in the privacy of their own bosoms lest they should discourage the hearts of their brethren.

HANNAH WHITALL SMITH

Celebrating Others

Let us think about each other and help each other to show love and do good deeds.

HEBREWS 10:24 NCV

Do you delight in the victories of others? You should. Each day provides countless opportunities to encourage others and to praise their good works. When you do so, you not only spread seeds of joy and happiness, you also obey the commandments of God's Holy Word.

Life is a team sport, and all of us need occasional pats on the back from our teammates. As Christians, we are called upon to spread the Good News of Christ, and we are also called to spread a message of encouragement and hope to the world.

Today, let us be cheerful Christians with smiles on our faces and encouraging words on our lips. By blessing others, we also bless ourselves, and, at the same time, we do honor to the One who gave His life for us.

A hug is the ideal gift . . . one size fits all.

ANONYMOUS

Family Life

Choose for yourselves this day whom you will serve . . . .
But as for me and my house, we will serve the Lord.

JOSHUA 24:15 NKJV

As every woman knows, family life is a mixture of conversations, mediations, irritations, deliberations, commiserations, frustrations, negotiations and celebrations. In other words, the life of the typical mom is incredibly varied.

Certainly, in the life of every family, there are moments of frustration and disappointment. Lots of them. But, for those who are lucky enough to live in the presence of a close-knit, caring clan, the rewards far outweigh the frustrations. That's why we pray fervently for our family members, and that's why we love them despite their faults.

No family is perfect, and neither is yours. But, despite the inevitable challenges and occasional hurt feelings of family life, your clan is God's gift to you. That little band of men, women, kids, and babies is a priceless treasure on temporary loan from the Father above. Give thanks to the Giver for the gift of family . . . and act accordingly.

How Often Must We Forgive?

Then Peter came to him and asked, "Lord, how often should I forgive someone who sins against me? Seven times?" "No!" Jesus replied, "seventy times seven!"

MATTHEW 18:21-22 NLT

How often must we forgive family members and friends? More times than we can count. Our children are precious but imperfect; so are our spouses and our friends. We must, on occasion, forgive those who have injured us; to do otherwise is to disobey God.

Are you easily frustrated by the inevitable imperfections of others? Are you a prisoner of bitterness and regret? If so, perhaps you need a refresher course in the art of forgiveness.

If there exists even one person, alive or dead, whom you have not forgiven (and that includes yourself), follow God's commandment and His will for your life: forgive. Bitterness, anger, and regret are not part of God's plan for your life. Forgiveness is.

How often should you forgive the other person? Only as many times as you want God to forgive you!

MARIE T. FREEMAN

Using Our Gifts

Based on the gift they have received, everyone should use it to serve others, as good managers of the varied grace of God.

1 PETER 4:10 HCSB

How do we thank God for the gifts He has given us? By using those gifts for the glory of His kingdom.

God has given you talents and opportunities that are uniquely yours. Are you willing to use your gifts in the way that God intends? And are you willing to summon the discipline that is required to develop your talents and to hone your skills? That's precisely what God wants you to do, and that's precisely what you should desire for yourself.

As you seek to expand your talents, you will undoubtedly encounter stumbling blocks along the way, such as the fear of rejection or the fear of failure. When you do, don't stumble! Just continue to refine your skills, and offer your services to God. And when the time is right, He will use you—but it's up to you to be thoroughly prepared when He does.

God's Eternal Presence

And the world with its lust is passing away, but the one who does God's will remains forever.

1 JOHN 2:17 HCSB

God's hand is ever-present and everlasting. It has created the universe—and everything in it—out of nothingness. God's hand is everywhere you have ever been, and it is everywhere you will ever be. Your obligation, as a believer, is to reach out to Him and accept the peace, the love, the abundance, and the grace that He has offered.

Are you tired? Discouraged? Fearful? Be comforted. God's hand is with you. Are you worried or anxious? Be confident in God's power. He will never desert you. Are you grieving? Know that God understands your suffering. And rest assured that He will comfort you and that, in time, He will dry your tears.

Throughout every season of life, in times of celebration or sorrow, in times of victory or defeat, God's hand is not just near; it is always here. So why not reach out to Him right now?

He is more within us than we are ourselves.

ELIZABETH ANN SETON

Whose Way?

We can make our plans, but the LORD determines our steps.

PROVERBS 16:9 NLT

The popular song "My Way" is a perfectly good tune, but it's not a perfect guide for life-here-on-earth. If you're looking for life's perfect prescription, you'd better forget about doing things your way and start doing things God's way. The most important decision of your life is, of course, your commitment to accept Jesus Christ as your personal Lord and Savior. And once your eternal destiny is secured, you will undoubtedly ask yourself the question "What now, Lord?" If you earnestly seek God's will for your life, you will find it . . . in time.

Sometimes, God's plans are crystal clear; sometimes they are not. So be patient, keep searching, and keep praying. If you do, then in time, God will answer your prayers and make His plans known. You'll discover those plans by doing things His way . . . and you'll be eternally grateful that you did.

God wants us to serve Him with a willing spirit, one that would choose no other way.

BETH MOORE

Your Spiritual Journey

Dear brothers and sisters, whenever trouble comes your way, let it be an opportunity for joy. For when your faith is tested, your endurance has a chance to grow. So let it grow, for when your endurance is fully developed, you will be strong in character and ready for anything.

JAMES 1:2-4 NLT

The journey toward spiritual maturity lasts a lifetime. As Christians, we can and should continue to grow in the love and the knowledge of our Savior as long as we live. Norman Vincent Peale had the following advice for believers of all ages: "Ask the God who made you to keep remaking you." That advice, of course, is perfectly sound, but often ignored.

When we cease to grow, either emotionally or spiritually, we do ourselves a profound disservice. But, if we study God's Word, if we obey His commandments, and if we live in the center of His will, we will not be "stagnant" believers; we will, instead, be growing Christians . . . and that's exactly what God wants for our lives.

Wisdom enlarges our capacity for discovery and delight, causing wonder to grow as we grow.

SUSAN LENZKES

Our Best Friend

No one has greater love than this, that someone would lay down his life for his friends.

John 15:13 HCSB

Who's the best friend this world has ever had? Jesus, of course. And when you form a life-changing relationship with Him, He will be your best friend, too . . . your friend forever.

Jesus has offered to share the gifts of everlasting life and everlasting love with the world and with you. If you make mistakes, He'll stand by you. If you fall short of His commandments, He'll still love you. If you feel lonely or worried, He can touch your heart and lift your spirits.

Jesus wants you to enjoy a happy, healthy, abundant life. He wants you to walk with Him and to share His Good News. You can do it. And with a friend like Jesus, you will.

Jesus was the Savior who would deliver them not only from the bondage of sin but also from meaningless wandering through life.

Anne Graham Lotz

Another Day, Countless Opportunities

Therefore, as we have opportunity, we must work for the good of all, especially for those who belong to the household of faith.

GALATIANS 6:10 HCSB

Each day, as we awaken from sleep and begin the new day, we are confronted with countless opportunities to serve God and to worship Him. When we do, He blesses us. But, if we turn our backs to the Creator, or, if we are simply too busy to acknowledge His greatness, we do ourselves a profound disservice.

As women in a fast-changing world, we face challenges that sometimes leave us feeling overworked, over-committed, and overwhelmed. But God has different plans for us. He intends that we take time each day to slow down long enough to praise Him and glorify His Son. When we do, our spirits are calmed and our lives are enriched, as are the lives of our families and friends.

Each day provides a glorious opportunity to place ourselves in the service of the One who is the Giver of all blessings. May we seek His will, trust His word, and place Him where He belongs: at the center of our lives.

Who Are Our Neighbors?

Never walk away from someone who deserves help; your hand is God's hand for that person.

PROVERBS 3:27 MSG

Who are our neighbors? Jesus answered that question with the story of the Good Samaritan. Our neighbors are any people whom God places in our paths, especially those in need.

We know that we are instructed to love our neighbors, and yet there's so little time . . . and we're so busy. No matter. As Christians, we are commanded by our Lord and Savior to love our neighbors just as we love ourselves. Period.

This very day, you will encounter someone who needs a word of encouragement, or a pat on the back, or a helping hand, or a heartfelt prayer. And, if you don't reach out to that person, who will? If you don't take the time to understand the needs of your neighbors, who will? If you don't love your brothers and sisters, who will? So, today, look for a neighbor in need . . . and then do something to help. Father's orders.

Making God's Priorities Your Priorities

Lord, teach me your demands, and I will keep them until the end.

PSALM 119:33 NCV

Sometimes, amid the demands of daily life, we lose perspective. Life seems out of balance, and the pressures of everyday living seem overwhelming. What's needed is a fresh perspective, a restored sense of balance . . . and God.

If a temporary loss of perspective has left you worried, exhausted, or both, it's time to readjust your thought patterns. Negative thoughts are habit-forming; thankfully, so are positive ones. With practice, you can form the habit of focusing on God's priorities and your possibilities. When you do, you'll soon discover that you will spend less time fretting about your challenges and more time praising God for His gifts.

When you call upon the Lord and prayerfully seek His will, He will give you wisdom and perspective. When you make God's priorities your priorities, He will direct your steps and calm your fears. So today and every day hereafter, pray for a sense of balance and perspective. And remember: your thoughts are intensely powerful things, so handle them with care.

Prayer Now

Rejoice in hope; be patient in affliction; be persistent in prayer.

ROMANS 12:12 HCSB

Prayer is a powerful tool for communicating with our Creator; it is an opportunity to commune with the Giver of all things good. Prayer is not a thing to be taken lightly or to be used infrequently. Prayer should never be reserved for mealtimes or for bedtimes; it should be an ever-present focus in our daily lives.

In his first letter to the Thessalonians, Paul wrote, "Rejoice evermore. Pray without ceasing. In every thing give thanks: for this is the will of God in Christ Jesus concerning you" (vv. 5:17-18 KJV). Paul's words apply to every Christian of every generation.

Today, instead of turning things over in our minds, let us turn them over to God in prayer. Instead of worrying about our decisions, let's trust God to help us make them. Today, let us pray constantly about things great and small. God is listening, and He wants to hear from us. Now.

There will be no power in our lives apart from prayer.

ANGELA THOMAS

What to Do?

The lines of purpose in your lives never grow slack, tightly tied as they are to your future in heaven, kept taut by hope.

COLOSSIANS 1:5 MSG

"What on earth does God intend for me to do with my life?" It's an easy question to ask but, for many of us, a difficult question to answer. Why? Because God's purposes aren't always clear to us. Sometimes we wander aimlessly in a wilderness of our own making. And sometimes, we struggle mightily against God in an unsuccessful attempt to find success and happiness through our own means, not His.

Sometimes, God's intentions will be clear to you; other times, God's plan will seem uncertain at best. But even on those difficult days when you are unsure which way to turn, you must never lose sight of these overriding facts: God created you for a reason; He has important work for you to do; and He's waiting patiently for you to do it.

And the next step is up to you.

You're the only one who can do what you do.

LOIS EVANS

Your Own Worst Critic?

A devout life does bring wealth, but it's the rich simplicity of being yourself before God.

1 TIMOTHY 6:6 MSG

Are you your own worst critic? If so, it's time to become a little more understanding of the woman you see whenever you look into the mirror.

Millions of words have been written about various ways to improve self-image and increase self-esteem. Yet, maintaining a healthy self-image is, to a surprising extent, a matter of doing three things: 1. behaving ourselves 2. thinking healthy thoughts 3. finding a purpose for your life that pleases your Creator and yourself.

The Bible affirms the importance of self-acceptance by teaching Christians to love others as they love themselves (Matthew 22:37-40). God accepts us just as we are. And, if He accepts us—faults and all—then who are we to believe otherwise?

One of Satan's most effective ploys is to make us believe that we are small, insignificant, and worthless.

SUSAN LENZKES

Your Journey Continues

I've told you these things for a purpose: that my joy might be your joy, and your joy wholly mature.

JOHN 15:11 MSG

Complete spiritual maturity is never achieved in a day, or in a year, or even in a lifetime. The journey toward spiritual maturity is an ongoing process that continues, day by day, throughout every stage of life. Every stage of life has its opportunities and its challenges, and if we're wise, we continue to seek God's guidance as each new chapter of life unfolds. Norman Vincent Peale advised: "Ask the God who made you to keep remaking you." That counsel is perfectly sound, but easy to ignore.

When we cease to grow, either emotionally or spiritually, we do ourselves a profound disservice. But, if we focus our thoughts—and attune our hearts—to the will of God, we will make each day another stage in the spiritual journey . . . and that's precisely what God intends for us to do.

Have You Thanked Him Today?

And whatever you do, in word or in deed, do everything in the name of the Lord Jesus, giving thanks to God the Father through Him.

COLOSSIANS 3:17 HCSB

The words of 1 Thessalonians 5:18 remind us to give thanks in every circumstance of life. But sometimes, when our hearts are troubled and our spirits are crushed, we don't feel like celebrating. Yet even when the clouds of despair darken our lives, God offers us His love, His strength, and His grace. And as believers, we must thank Him.

Have you thanked God today for blessings that are too numerous to count? Have you offered Him your heartfelt prayers and your wholehearted praise? If not, it's time slow down and to offer a prayer of thanksgiving to the One who has given you life on earth and life eternal.

No matter our circumstances, we owe God so much more than we can ever repay, and the least we can do is to thank Him.

His Truth

And you shall know the truth, and the truth shall make you free.

JOHN 8:32 NKJV

God is vitally concerned with truth. His Word teaches the truth; His Spirit reveals the truth; His Son leads us to the truth. When we open our hearts to God, and when we allow His Son to rule over our thoughts and our lives, God reveals Himself, and we come to understand the truth about ourselves and the Truth (with a capital T) about God's gift of grace.

The familiar words of John 8:32 remind us that when we come to know God's Truth, we are liberated. Have you been liberated by that Truth? And are you living in accordance with the eternal truths that you find in God's Holy Word? Hopefully so.

Today, as you fulfill the responsibilities that God has placed before you, ask yourself this question: "Do my thoughts and actions bear witness to the ultimate Truth that God has placed in my heart, or am I allowing the pressures of everyday life to overwhelm me?" It's a profound question that deserves an answer . . . now.

Lots to Learn

Know that wisdom is sweet to your soul; if you find it, there is a future hope for you, and your hope will not be cut off.

PROVERBS 24:14 NIV

Whether you're twenty-two or a hundred and two, you've still got lots to learn. Even if you're a very wise person, God isn't finished with you yet. Why? Because lifetime learning is part of God's plan—and He certainly hasn't finished teaching you some very important lessons.

Do you seek to live a life of righteousness and wisdom? If so, you must continue to study the ultimate source of wisdom: the Word of God. You must associate, day in and day out, with godly men and women. And, you must act in accordance with your beliefs. When you study God's Word and live according to His commandments, you will become wise . . . and you will be a blessing to your friends, to your family, and to the world.

Knowledge is horizontal. Wisdom is vertical; it comes down from above.

BILLY GRAHAM

Don't Be Worried . . . You Are Protected

*But seek first his kingdom and his righteousness, and all
these things will be given to you as well. Therefore do not
worry about tomorrow, for tomorrow will worry about
itself. Each day has enough trouble of its own.*

MATTHEW 6:33-34 NIV

Because we are fallible human beings, we worry.
Even though we, as Christians, have the assurance
of salvation—even though we, as Christians, have the
promise of God's love and protection—we find ourselves
fretting over the countless details of everyday life.

If you are like most women, you may, on occasion,
find yourself worrying about health, about finances,
about safety, about relationships, about family, and
about countless other challenges of life, some great
and some small. Where is the best place to take your
worries? Take them to God. Take your troubles to Him,
and your fears, and your sorrows. And remember: God
is trustworthy . . . and you are protected.

Anxiety may be natural and normal for the world, but it
is not to be part of a believer's lifestyle.

KAY ARTHUR

The Donut and the Hole

Be careful what you think, because your thoughts run your life.

PROVERBS 4:23 NCV

On the wall of a little donut shop, the sign said: As you travel through life, brother, whatever be your goal, keep your eye upon the donut, and not upon the hole.

Are you a Christian who keeps your eye upon the donut, or have you acquired the bad habit of looking only at the hole? Hopefully, you spend most of your waking hours looking at the donut (and thanking God for it).

Christianity and pessimism don't mix. So do yourself a favor: choose to be a hope-filled Christian. Think optimistically about your life and your future. Trust your hopes, not your fears. Take time to celebrate God's glorious creation. And then, when you've filled your heart with hope and gladness, share your optimism with your friends. They'll be better for it, and so will you. But not necessarily in that order.

Don't miss the beautiful colors of the rainbow while you're looking for the pot of gold at the end of it!

BARBARA JOHNSON

Filled by the Spirit

I will put my Spirit in you and you will live . . . .
 EZEKIEL 37:14 NIV

Are you burdened by the pressures of everyday living? If so, it's time to take the pressure off. How can you do so? By allowing the Holy Spirit to fill you and do His work in your life.

When you are filled with the Holy Spirit, your words and deeds will reflect a love and devotion to Christ. When you are filled with the Holy Spirit, the steps of your life's journey are guided by the Lord. When you allow God's Spirit to work in you and through you, you will be energized and transformed.

Today, allow yourself to be filled with the Spirit of God. And then stand back in amazement as God begins to work miracles in your own life and in the lives of those you love.

The Holy Spirit is the secret of the power in my life. All I have to do is surrender my life to Him.

KATHRYN KUHLMAN

I feel my weakness and inability to accomplish anything without the aid of the Holy Spirit.

LOTTIE MOON

God Is the Giver

I came that they may have life, and have it abundantly.
JOHN 10:10 NASB

The familiar words of John 10:10 should serve as a daily reminder: Christ came to this earth so that we might experience His abundance, His love, and His gift of eternal life. But Christ does not force Himself upon us; we must claim His gifts for ourselves.

Every woman knows that some days are so busy and so hurried that abundance seems a distant promise. It is not. Every day, we can claim the spiritual abundance that God promises for our lives . . . and we should.

Hannah Whitall Smith spoke for believers of every generation when she observed, "God is the giver, and we are the receivers. And His richest gifts are bestowed not upon those who do the greatest things, but upon those who accept His abundance and His grace."

Christ is, indeed, the Giver. Will you accept His gifts today?

If we just give God the little that we have, we can trust Him to make it go around.

GLORIA GAITHER

Beyond Foolish Arguments

But stay away from those who have foolish arguments and talk about useless family histories and argue and quarrel about the law. Those things are worth nothing and will not help anyone.

TITUS 3:9 NCV

Arguments are seldom won but often lost. When we engage in petty squabbles, our losses usually outpace our gains. When we acquire the unfortunate habit of habitual bickering, we do harm to our friends, to our families, to our coworkers, and to ourselves.

Time and again, God's Word warns us that most arguments are a monumental waste of time, of energy, of life. In Titus, we are warned to refrain from "foolish arguments," and with good reason. Such arguments usually do more for the devil than they do for God.

So the next time you're tempted to engage in a silly squabble, whether inside the church or outside it, refrain. When you do, you'll put a smile on God's face, and you'll send the devil packing.

You don't have to attend every argument you're invited to!

ANONYMOUS

Sharing Your Burdens

The LORD himself goes before you and will be with you; he will never leave you nor forsake you. Do not be afraid; do not be discouraged.

DEUTERONOMY 31:8 NIV

The Bible promises this: tough times are temporary but God's love is not—God's love endures forever. So what does that mean to you? Just this: From time to time, everybody faces hardships and disappointments, and so will you. And when tough times arrive, God always stands ready to protect you and to heal you. Your task is straightforward: you must share your burdens with Him.

As Corrie ten Boom observed, "Any concern that is too small to be turned into a prayer is too small to be made into a burden." Those are comforting words, especially in these difficult days.

Whatever the size of your challenges, God is big enough to handle them. Ask for His help today, with faith and with fervor. Instead of turning things over in your mind, turn them over to God in prayer. Instead of worrying about your next decision, ask God to lead the way. Cast your burdens upon the One who cannot be shaken, and rest assured that He always hears your prayers.

Choices, Choices, Choices

Don't depend on your own wisdom. Respect the Lord and refuse to do wrong.

Life is a series of decisions and choices. Each day, we make countless decisions that can bring us closer to God . . . or not. When we live according to God's commandments, we earn for ourselves the abundance and peace that He intends for our lives. But, when we turn our backs upon God by disobeying Him, we bring needless suffering upon ourselves and our families.

Do you seek spiritual abundance that can be yours through the person of God's only begotten Son? Then invite Christ into your heart and live according to His teachings. And, when you confront a difficult decision or a powerful temptation, seek God's wisdom and trust it. When you do, you will receive untold blessings—not only for this day, but also for all eternity.

Choices can change our lives profoundly. The choice to mend a broken relationship, to say "yes" to a difficult assignment, to lay aside some important work to play with a child, to visit some forgotten person—these small choices may affect many lives eternally.

Gloria Gaither

Beyond the Crises

But the wisdom that is from above is first pure, then peaceable, gentle, willing to yield, full of mercy and good fruits, without partiality and without hypocrisy.

JAMES 3:17 NKJV

Your decision to seek a deeper relationship with God will not remove all problems from your life; to the contrary, it will bring about a series of personal crises as you constantly seek to say "yes" to God although the world encourages you to do otherwise. You live in a world that seeks to snare your attention and lead you away from God. Each time you are tempted to distance yourself from the Creator, you will face a spiritual crisis. A few of these crises may be monumental in scope, but most will be the small, everyday decisions of life. In fact, life here on earth can be seen as one test after another— and with each crisis comes yet another opportunity to grow closer to God . . . or to distance yourself from His plan for your life.

Today, you will face many opportunities to say "yes" to your Creator—and you will also encounter many opportunities to say "no" to Him. Your answers will determine the quality of your day and the direction of your life, so answer carefully . . . very carefully.

Big Dreams

With God's power working in us, God can do much, much more than anything we can ask or imagine.

EPHESIANS 3:20 NCV

She was born in rural Mississippi and lived with her grandmother in a house that had no indoor plumbing. She made it to college in Nashville, where she got her start in television. Over time, she moved to the top of her profession, and today, her show, *Oprah*, is an unparalleled hit.

When questioned about her journey to the top, Oprah said, "God can dream a bigger dream than we can dream for ourselves." She was right. So try Oprah's formula: increase the size of your dreams. Because the Good Lord's plan for each of us is big, very big. But it's up to us to accept the part, to step up on stage and to perform.

The future lies all before us. Shall it only be a slight advance upon what we usually do? Ought it not to be a bound, a leap forward to altitudes of endeavor and success undreamed of before?

ANNIE ARMSTRONG

What Kind of Example?

You are the light that gives light to the world . . . . In the same way, you should be a light for other people. Live so that they will see the good things you do and will praise your Father in heaven.

MATTHEW 5:14,16 NCV

Whether we like it or not, all of us are examples. The question is not whether we will be examples to our families and friends; the question is simply what kind of examples will we be.

What kind of example are you? Are you the kind of woman whose life serves as a powerful example of righteousness? Are you a woman whose behavior serves as a positive role model for young people? Are you the kind of woman whose actions, day in and day out, are based upon integrity, fidelity, and a love for the Lord? If so, you are not only blessed by God, you are also a powerful force for good in a world that desperately needs positive influences such as yours.

D. L. Moody advised, "A man ought to live so that everybody knows he is a Christian, and most of all, his family ought to know." And that's sound advice because our families and friends are watching . . . and so, for that matter, is God.

Is Christ the Focus?

I do not consider myself to have taken hold of it. But one thing I do: forgetting what is behind and reaching forward to what is ahead, I pursue as my goal the prize promised by God's heavenly call in Christ Jesus.

PHILIPPIANS 3:13-14 HCSB

Is Christ the focus of your life? Are you fired up with enthusiasm for Him? Are you an energized Christian who allows God's Son to reign over every aspect of your day? Make no mistake: that's exactly what God intends for you to do.

God has given you the gift of eternal life through His Son. In response to God's priceless gift, you are instructed to focus your thoughts, your prayers, and your energies upon God and His only begotten Son. To do so, you must resist the subtle yet powerful temptation to become a "spiritual dabbler."

A person who dabbles in the Christian faith is unwilling to place God in His rightful place: above all other things. Resist that temptation; make God the cornerstone and the touchstone of your life. When you do, He will give you all the strength and wisdom you need to live victoriously for Him.

Finding Fulfillment

You haven't done this before. Ask, using my name, and you will receive, and you will have abundant joy.

JOHN 16:24 NLT

Everywhere we turn, or so it seems, the world promises fulfillment, contentment, and happiness. But the contentment that the world offers is fleeting and incomplete. Thankfully, the fulfillment that God offers is all encompassing and everlasting.

Happiness depends less upon our circumstances than our thoughts. When we turn our thoughts to God, to His gifts, and to His glorious creation, we experience the joy that God intends for His children. But, when we focus on the negative aspects of life—or when we disobey God's commandments—we cause ourselves needless suffering.

Sometimes, amid the inevitable hustle and bustle of daily life, we can forfeit—albeit temporarily—the joy of Christ as we wrestle with the challenges of daily living. Yet God's Word is clear: fulfillment through Christ is available to all who seek it and claim it. Count yourself among that number. Seek first a personal, transforming relationship with Jesus, and then claim the joy, the fulfillment, and the spiritual abundance that the Shepherd offers His sheep.

His Will and Ours

Blessed are those servants, whom the lord when he cometh shall find watching....

God has will, and so do we. He gave us the power to make choices for ourselves, and He created a world in which those choices have consequences. The ultimate choice that we face, of course, is what to do about God. We can cast our lot with Him by choosing Jesus Christ as our personal Savior, or not. The choice is ours alone.

We also face thousands of small choices that make up the fabric of daily life. When we align those choices with God's commandments, and when we align our lives with God's will, we receive His abundance, His peace, and His joy. But when we struggle against God's will for our lives, we reap a bitter harvest indeed.

Today, you'll face thousands of small choices; as you do, use God's Word as your guide. And, as you face the ultimate choice, place God's Son and God's will and God's love at the center of your life. You'll discover that God's plan is far grander than any you could have imagined.

Your Relationship with God

Unfailing love surrounds those who trust the LORD.

St. Augustine observed, "God loves each of us as if there were only one of us." Do you believe those words? Do you seek to have an intimate, one-on-one relationship with your Heavenly Father, or are you satisfied to keep Him at a "safe" distance?

Sometimes, in the crush of our daily duties, God may seem far away, but He is not. God is everywhere we have ever been and everywhere we will ever go. He is with us night and day; He knows our thoughts and our prayers. And, when we earnestly seek Him, we will find Him because He is here, waiting patiently for us to reach out to Him.

Let us reach out to Him today and always. And let us praise Him for the glorious gifts that have transformed us today and forever. Amen.

I have learned that the more we understand how very much God loves us, and the more we comprehend the grace He has demonstrated toward us, the more humble we become.

SERITA ANN JAKES

Beyond Confusion

Trust the Lord with all your heart, and don't depend on your own understanding. Remember the Lord in all you do, and he will give you success.

PROVERBS 3:5-6 NCV

The Bible contains promises, made by God, upon which we, as believers, can and must depend. But sometimes, especially when we find ourselves caught in the inevitable entanglements of life, we fail to trust God completely.

Are you tired? Discouraged? Fearful? Be comforted and trust the promises that God has made to you. Are you worried or anxious? Be confident in God's power. Do you see a difficult future ahead? Be courageous and call upon God. He will protect you and then use you according to His purposes. Are you confused? Listen to the quiet voice of your Heavenly Father. He is not a God of confusion. Talk with Him; listen to Him; trust Him, and trust His promises. He is steadfast, and He is your Protector . . . forever.

When the winds are cold, and the days are long, and thy soul from care would hide, fly back, fly back, to thy Father then, and beneath His wings abide.

FANNY CROSBY

Trusting His Timing

Therefore humble yourselves under the mighty hand of God, that He may exalt you in due time.

1 Peter 5:6 NKJV

If you sincerely seek to be a woman of faith, then you must learn to trust God's timing. You will be sorely tempted, however, to do otherwise. Because you are a fallible human being, you are impatient for things to happen. But, God knows better.

God has created a world that unfolds according to His own timetable, not ours . . . thank goodness! We mortals might make a terrible mess of things. God does not.

God's plan does not always happen in the way that we would like or at the time of our own choosing. Our task—as believing Christians who trust in a benevolent, all-knowing Father—is to wait patiently for God to reveal Himself. And reveal Himself He will. Always. But until God's perfect plan is made known, we must walk in faith and never lose hope. And we must continue to trust Him. Always.

Waiting is an essential part of spiritual discipline. It can be the ultimate test of faith.

Anne Graham Lotz

Wisdom and Hope

Know that wisdom is sweet to your soul; if you find it, there is a future hope for you, and your hope will not be cut off.

PROVERBS 24:14 NIV

Wisdom and hope are traveling companions. Wise men and women learn to think optimistically about their lives, their futures, and their faith. The pessimists, however, are not so fortunate; they choose instead to focus their thoughts and energies on faultfinding, criticizing, and complaining, with precious little to show for their efforts.

To become wise, we must seek God's wisdom—the wisdom of hope—and we must live according to God's Word. To become wise, we must seek God's guidance with consistency and purpose. To become wise, we must not only learn the lessons of life, we must live by them.

Do you seek wisdom for yourself and for your family? Then remember this: The ultimate source of wisdom is the Word of God. When you study God's Word and live according to His commandments, you will grow wise, you will remain hopeful, and you will be a blessing to your family and to the world.

Kindness in Action

Yes indeed, it is good when you truly obey our Lord's royal command found in the Scriptures: "Love your neighbor as yourself."

JAMES 2:8 NLT

The words of Matthew 7:12 remind us that, as believers in Christ, we are commanded to treat others as we wish to be treated. This commandment is, indeed, the Golden Rule for Christians of every generation.

Kindness is a choice. Sometimes, when we feel happy or prosperous, we find it easy to be kind. Other times, when we are discouraged or tired, we can scarcely summon the energy to utter a single kind word. But, God's commandment is clear: we must observe the Golden Rule "in everything." God intends that we make the conscious choice to treat others with kindness and respect, no matter our circumstances, no matter our emotions. Kindness, therefore, is a choice that we, as Christians must make many times each day.

When we weave the thread of kindness into the very fabric of our lives, we give a priceless gift to others, and we give glory to the One who gave His life for us. As believers, we must do no less.

He Is at Work

You are the God who works wonders; You revealed Your strength among the peoples.

PSALM 77:14 HCSB

Do you believe that God is at work in the world? And do you also believe that nothing is impossible for Him? If so, then you also believe that God is perfectly capable of doing things that you, as a mere human being with limited vision and limited understanding, would deem to be utterly impossible. And that's precisely what God does.

Since the moment that He created our universe out of nothingness, God has made a habit of doing miraculous things. And He still works miracles today. Expect Him to work miracles in your own life, and then be watchful. With God, absolutely nothing is impossible, including an amazing assortment of miracles that He stands ready, willing, and able to perform for you and yours.

Faith means believing in realities that go beyond sense and sight. It is the awareness of unseen divine realities all around you.

JONI EARECKSON TADA

Impatient?

Therefore the Lord is waiting to show you mercy, and is rising up to show you compassion, for the Lord is a just God. Happy are all who wait patiently for Him.

ISAIAH 30:18 HCSB

Most of us are impatient for God to grant us the desires of our heart. Usually, we know what we want, and we know precisely when we want it: right now, if not sooner. But God may have other plans. And when God's plans differ from our own, we must trust in His infinite wisdom and in His infinite love.

As busy men and women living in a fast-paced world, many of us find that waiting quietly for God is difficult. Why? Because we are fallible human beings seeking to live according to our own timetables, not God's. In our better moments, we realize that patience is not only a virtue, it is also a commandment from God.

God instructs us to be patient in all things. We must be patient with our families, our friends, and our associates. We must also be patient with our Creator as He unfolds His plan for our lives. And that's as it should be. After all, think how patient God has been with us.

Whom Should We Please?

*Our only goal is to please God whether we live here or there,
because we must all stand before Christ to be judged.*

2 CORINTHIANS 5:9-10 NCV

As a member-in-good-standing this highly competitive, 21st-century world, you know that the demands and expectations of everyday living can seem burdensome, even overwhelming at times. Keeping up with the Joneses can become a fulltime job if you let it. A better strategy, of course, is to stop trying to please the neighbors and to concentrate, instead, upon pleasing God.

Perhaps you have set your goals high; if so, congratulations! You're willing to dream big dreams, and that's a very good thing. But as you consider your life's purpose, don't allow your quest for excellence to interfere with the spiritual journey that God has planned for you.

As a believer, your instructions are clear: you must strive to please God. How do you please Him? By accepting His Son and obeying His commandments. All other concerns—including, but not limited to, keeping up with the Joneses—are of little or no importance.

Praising His Marvelous Works

Enter into His gates with thanksgiving, and into His courts with praise. Be thankful to Him, and bless His name. For the Lord is good; His mercy is everlasting, and His truth endures to all generations.

PSALM 100:4-5 NKJV

In the Hebrew version of the Old Testament, the title of the book of Psalms is translated "hymns of praise," and with good reason. Much of the book is a breathtakingly beautiful celebration of God's power, God's love, and God's creation. The psalmist writes, "Let everything that breathes praise the Lord. Hallelujah!" (150:6 HCSB).

As Christians, we should continually praise God for all that He has done and all that He will do. His works are marvelous, His gifts are beyond understanding, and His love endures forever.

Do you sincerely desire to be a worthy servant of the One who has given you eternal love and eternal life? Then praise Him. And don't just praise Him on Sunday morning. Praise Him all day long, every day, for as long as you live . . . and then for all eternity.

God is worthy of our praise and is pleased when we come before Him with thanksgiving.

SHIRLEY DOBSON

Beyond Procrastination

Now, Lord, what do I wait for? My hope is in You.
Psalm 39:7 HCSB

The habit of procrastination takes a two-fold toll on its victims. First, important work goes unfinished; second (and more importantly), valuable energy is wasted in the process of putting off the things that remain undone. Procrastination results from an individual's short-sighted attempt to postpone temporary discomfort. What results is a senseless cycle of 1. delay, followed by 2. worry followed by 3. a panicky and often futile attempt to "catch up." Procrastination is, at its core, a struggle against oneself; the only antidote is action.

Once you acquire the habit of doing what needs to be done when it needs to be done, you will avoid untold trouble, worry, and stress. So learn to defeat procrastination by paying less attention to your fears and more attention to your responsibilities. God has created a world that punishes procrastinators and rewards men and women who "do it now." In other words, life doesn't procrastinate. Neither should you.

Play It Safe?

Cast your burden upon the Lord and He will sustain you;
He will never allow the righteous to be shaken.

PSALM 55:22 NASB

As we consider the uncertainties of the future, we are confronted with a powerful temptation: the temptation to "play it safe." Unwilling to move mountains, we fret over molehills. Unwilling to entertain great hopes for tomorrow, we focus on the unfairness of today. Unwilling to trust God completely, we take timid half-steps when God intends that we make giant leaps.

Today, ask God for the courage to step beyond the boundaries of your doubts. Ask Him to guide you to a place where you can realize your full potential—a place where you are freed from the fear of failure. Ask Him to do His part, and promise Him that you will do your part. Don't ask Him to lead you to a "safe" place; ask Him to lead you to the "right" place . . . and remember: those two places are seldom the same.

I believe that God meant for life to take our breath away, sometimes because of the sheer joy of it all and sometimes because of the severe pain. To choose living over pretending means that we will know both.

ANGELA THOMAS

Disobedience Invites Disaster

*If you hide your sins, you will not succeed. If you confess
and reject them, you will receive mercy.*

PROVERBS 28:13 NCV

As creatures of free will, we may disobey God whenever we choose, but when we do so, we put ourselves and our loved ones in peril. Why? Because disobedience invites disaster. We cannot sin against God without consequence. We cannot live outside His will without injury. We cannot distance ourselves from God without hardening our hearts. We cannot yield to the ever-tempting distractions of our world and, at the same time, enjoy God's peace.

Sometimes, in a futile attempt to justify our behaviors, we make a distinction between "big" sins and "little" ones. To do so is a mistake of "big" proportions. Sins of all shapes and sizes have the power to do us great harm. And in a world where sin is big business, that's certainly a sobering thought.

Sin is largely a matter of mistaken priorities. Any sin in us that is cherished, hidden, and not confessed will cut the nerve center of our faith.

CATHERINE MARSHALL

Your Unique Talents

Now there are varieties of gifts, but the same Spirit. And there are varieties of ministries, and the same Lord.

1 CORINTHIANS 12:4-5 NASB

God has given you an array of talents, and He has given you unique opportunities to share those talents with the world. Your Creator intends for you to use your talents for the glory of His kingdom in the service of His children. Will you honor Him by sharing His gifts? And, will you share His gifts humbly and lovingly? Hopefully you will.

The old saying is both familiar and true: "What you are is God's gift to you; what you become is your gift to God." As a woman who has been touched by the transforming love of Jesus Christ, your obligation is clear: You must strive to make the most of your own God-given talents, and you must encourage your family and friends to do likewise.

Today, make this promise to yourself and to God: Promise to use your talents to minister to your family, to your friends, and to the world. And remember: The best way to say "Thank You" for God's gifts is to use them.

Night Is Coming

I must work the works of Him who sent Me while it is day;
the night is coming when no one can work.

JOHN 9:4 NKJV

The words of John 9:4 remind us that "night is coming" for all of us. But until then, God gives us each day and fills it to the brim with possibilities. The day is presented to us fresh and clean at midnight, free of charge, but we must beware: Today is a nonrenewable resource—once it's gone, it's gone forever. Our responsibility, of course, is to use this day in the service of God's will and in accordance with His commandments.

Today, treasure the time that God has given you. And search for the hidden possibilities that God has placed along your path. This day is a priceless gift from your Creator, so use it joyfully and productively. And encourage others to do likewise. After all, night is coming when no one can work . . .

Live today fully, expressing gratitude for all you have been, all you are right now, and all you are becoming.

MELODIE BEATTIE

When We Face Adversity

When you go through deep waters and great trouble, I will be with you. When you go through the rivers of difficulty, you will not drown! When you walk through the fire of oppression, you will not be burned up; the flames will not consume you. For I am the Lord, your God . . . .

Isaiah 43:2-3 NLT

From time to time, all of us face adversity, discouragement, or disappointment. And, throughout life, we must all endure life-changing personal losses that leave us breathless. When we do, God stands ready to protect us. Psalm 147 promises, "He heals the brokenhearted, and binds their wounds" (v. 3, NIV).

When we are troubled, we must call upon God, and, in His own time and according to His own plan, He will heal us.

Are you anxious? Take those anxieties to God. Are you troubled? Take your troubles to Him. Does your world seem to be trembling beneath your feet? Seek protection from the One who cannot be moved. The same God who created the universe will protect you if you ask Him . . . so ask Him.

Actions and Beliefs

If the way you live isn't consistent with what you believe, then it's wrong.

ROMANS 14:23 MSG

We must do our best to make sure that our actions are accurate reflections of our beliefs. Our theology must be demonstrated, not only by our words but, more importantly, by our actions. In short, we should be practical women, quick to act upon the beliefs that we hold most dear.

We may proclaim our beliefs to our hearts' content, but our proclamations will mean nothing—to others or to ourselves—unless we accompany our words with deeds that match. The sermons that we live are far more compelling than the ones we preach.

Like it or not, your life is an accurate reflection of your creed. If this fact gives you cause for concern, don't bother talking about the changes that you intend to make—make them. Now.

We are to leave an impression on all those we meet that communicates whose we are and what kingdom we represent.

LISA BEVERE

When It's Time for a Different Plan

But as for you, be strong; don't be discouraged, for your work has a reward.

2 CHRONICLES 15:7 HCSB

Some of our most important dreams are the ones we abandon. Some of our most important goals are the ones we don't attain. Sometimes, our most important journeys are the ones that we take to the winding conclusion of what seem to be dead end streets. Thankfully, with God there are no dead ends; there are only opportunities to learn, to yield, to trust, to serve, and to grow.

The next time you experience one of life's inevitable disappointments, don't despair and don't be afraid to try "Plan B." Consider every setback an opportunity to choose a different, more appropriate path. Have faith that God may indeed be leading you in an entirely different direction, a direction of His choosing. And as you take your next step, remember that what looks like a dead end to you may, in fact, be the fast lane according to God.

God uses our most stumbling, faltering faith-steps as the open door to His doing for us "more than we ask or think."

CATHERINE MARSHALL

Finding Contentment

I know what it is to be in need, and I know what it is to have plenty. I have learned the secret of being content in any and every situation, whether well fed or hungry, whether living in plenty or in want. I can do everything through him who gives me strength.

PHILIPPIANS 4:12-13 NIV

The preoccupation with happiness and contentment is an ever-present theme in the modern world. We are bombarded with messages that tell us where to find peace and pleasure in a world that worships materialism and wealth. But, lasting contentment is not found in material possessions; genuine contentment is a spiritual gift from God to those who trust in Him and follow His commandments.

Where do we find contentment? If we don't find it in God, we will never find it anywhere else. But, if we put our faith and our trust in Him, we will be blessed with an inner peace that is beyond human understanding. When God dwells at the center of our lives, peace and contentment will belong to us just as surely as we belong to God.

Discipleship Now

You did not choose Me, but I chose you. I appointed you that you should go out and produce fruit, and that your fruit should remain, so that whatever you ask the Father in My name, He will give you.

JOHN 15:16 HCSB

When Jesus addressed His disciples, He warned that each one must, "take up his cross and follow Me." The disciples must have known exactly what the Master meant. In Jesus' day, prisoners were forced to carry their own crosses to the location where they would be put to death. Thus, Christ's message was clear: in order to follow Him, Christ's disciples must deny themselves and, instead, trust Him completely. Nothing has changed since then.

If we are to be disciples of Christ, we must trust Him and place Him at very center of our beings. Jesus never comes "next." He is always first. The paradox, of course, is that only by sacrificing ourselves to Him do we gain salvation for ourselves.

Do you seek to be a worthy disciple of Christ? Then pick up His cross today and every day that you live. When you do, He will bless you now and forever.

Hope Is Contagious

A word spoken at the right time is like golden apples on a silver tray.

PROVERBS 25:11 HCSB

Hope, like other human emotions, is contagious. If you associate with hope-filled, enthusiastic people, their enthusiasm will have a tendency to lift your spirits. But if you find yourself spending too much time in the company of naysayers, pessimists, or cynics, your thoughts, like theirs, will tend to be negative.

Are you a hopeful, optimistic Christian? And do you associate with like-minded people? If so, then you're availing yourself of a priceless gift: the encouragement of fellow believers. But, if you find yourself focusing on the negative aspects of life, perhaps it is time to search out a few new friends.

As a faithful follower of the man from Galilee, you have every reason to be hopeful. So today, look for reasons to celebrate God's endless blessings. And while you're at it, look for people who will join with you in the celebration. You'll be better for their company, and they'll be better for yours.

Focusing on God

Give your entire attention to what God is doing right now, and don't get worked up about what may or may not happen tomorrow. God will help you deal with whatever hard things come up when the time comes.

MATTHEW 6:34 MSG

All of us may find our courage tested by the inevitable disappointments and tragedies of life. After all, ours is a world filled with uncertainty, hardship, sickness, and danger. Old Man Trouble, it seems, is never too far from the front door.

When we focus upon our fears and our doubts, we may find many reasons to lie awake at night and fret about the uncertainties of the coming day. A better strategy, of course, is to focus not upon our fears, but instead upon our God.

God is as near as your next breath, and He is in control. He offers salvation to all His children, including you. God is your shield and your strength; you are His forever. So don't focus your thoughts upon the fears of the day. Instead, trust God's plan and His eternal love for you. And remember: God is good, and He has the last word.

When It's Hard to Forgive

I can do all things through Christ, because he gives me strength.

PHILIPPIANS 4:13 NCV

Whenever people hurt us—whether emotionally, physically, financially, or otherwise—it's hard to forgive. But God's Word is clear: we must forgive other people, even when we'd rather not. So, if you're angry with anybody (or if you're upset by something you yourself have done) it's now time to forgive.

God instructs you to treat other people exactly as you wish to be treated. And since you want to be forgiven for the mistakes that you make, you must be willing to extend forgiveness to other people for the mistakes that they have made.

If you can't seem to forgive someone, you should keep asking God for help you until you do. And of this you can be sure: if you keep asking for God's help, He will give it.

Our relationships with other people are of primary importance to God. Because God is love, He cannot tolerate any unforgiveness or hardness in us toward any individual.

CATHERINE MARSHALL

Cultivating God's Gifts

I remind you to fan into flame the gift of God.

2 TIMOTHY 1:6 NIV

All women possess special gifts and talents; you are no exception. But, your gift is no guarantee of success; it must be cultivated and nurtured; otherwise, it will go unused . . . and God's gift to you will be squandered. Today, accept this challenge: value the talent that God has given you, nourish it, make it grow, and share it with the world. After all, the best way to say "Thank You" for God's gift is to use it.

Yes, we need to acknowledge our weaknesses, to confess our sins. But if we want to be active, productive participants in the realm of God, we also need to recognize our gifts, to appreciate our strengths, to build on the abilities God has given us. We need to balance humility with confidence.

PENELOPE STOKES

Garden Tip: All of God's gifts are good, and we should share His gifts with the world.

Always Faithful

Let us hold on to the confession of our hope without wavering, for He who promised is faithful.

HEBREWS 10:23 HCSB

The Bible makes it perfectly clear: the heart of God is always faithful. The faithfulness of God does not mean we, His children, are freed from life's problems and tragedies. It means that God will preserve us in our difficulties, not from our difficulties.

God's faithfulness is made clear in the beautiful words of Psalm 23:4: "Yea, though I walk through the valley of the shadow of death, I will fear no evil: for thou art with me; thy rod and thy staff they comfort me" (KJV). God does not exempt us from the valleys of life, but neither does He ask us to walk alone. He is always there.

God's heart is faithful. He's faithful to His people; He is faithful to His Word; and He is faithful to you. Paul writes in 1 Corinthians 1:9, "God is faithful, by whom you were called into the fellowship of His Son, Jesus Christ our Lord" (NKJV). God has a faithful heart. Trust Him, and take comfort in the unerring promises and the never-ending faithfulness of your Lord.

God's Plan, Our Responsibilities

His master said to him, "Well done, good and faithful slave! You were faithful over a few things; I will put you in charge of many things. Enter your master's joy!"

MATTHEW 25:21 HCSB

God has promised us this: when we do our duties in small matters, He will give us additional responsibilities. Sometimes, those responsibilities come when God changes the course of our lives so that we may better serve Him. Sometimes, our rewards come in the form of temporary setbacks that lead, in turn, to greater victories. Sometimes, God rewards us by answering "no" to our prayers so that He can say "yes" to a far grander request that we, with our limited understanding, would never have thought to ask for.

If you seek to be God's servant in great matters, be faithful, be patient, and be dutiful in smaller matters. Then step back and watch as God surprises you with the spectacular creativity of His infinite wisdom and His perfect plan.

I firmly believe that as we prove ourselves to be responsible with our resources, more and more resources will be entrusted to us to handle faithfully.

MARY HUNT

Still Growing

*When I was a child, I spoke and thought and reasoned
as a child does. But when I grew up, I put away childish
things.*

1 Corinthians 13:11 NLT

If we are to grow as women, we need both knowledge
and wisdom. Knowledge is found in textbooks.
Wisdom, on the other hand, is found through
experience, through years of trial and error, and through
careful attention to the Word of God. Knowledge is an
important building block in a well-lived life, and it pays
rich dividends both personally and professionally. But,
wisdom is even more important because it refashions
not only our minds, but also our hearts.

When it comes to your faith, God doesn't intend
for you to stand still. He wants you to keep growing as a
woman and as a spiritual being. No matter how "grown-
up" you may be, you still have growing to do. And the
more you grow, the more beautiful you become, inside
and out.

One of the marks of Spiritual maturity is a consistent,
Spirit-controlled life.

Vonette Bright

The Cornerstone

For the Son of Man has come to save that which was lost.
MATTHEW 18:11 NKJV

Is Jesus the cornerstone of your life . . . or have you relegated Him to a far corner of your life? The answer to this question will determine the quality, the direction, the tone, and the ultimate destination of your life here on earth and your life throughout eternity.

Thomas Brooks spoke for believers of every generation when he observed, "Christ is the sun, and all the watches of our lives should be set by the dial of his motion." Christ, indeed, is the ultimate Savior of mankind and the personal Savior of those who believe in Him. As His servants, we should place Him at the very center of our lives. And every day that God gives us breath, we should share Christ's love and His message with a world that needs both.

Jesus makes God visible as Man. He is the God-Man, God walking the earth in a human body, God robed in homespun, God come down!

ANNE GRAHAM LOTZ

Walking in the Light

I have come as a light into the world, that whoever believes in Me should not abide in darkness.

JOHN 12:46 NKJV

God's Holy Word instructs us that Jesus is, "the way, the truth, and the life" (John 14:6-7). Without Christ, we are as far removed from salvation as the east is removed from the west. And without Christ, we can never know the ultimate truth: God's truth.

Truth is God's way: He commands His believers to live in truth, and He rewards those who do so. Jesus is the personification of God's liberating truth, a truth that offers salvation to mankind.

Do you seek to walk with God? Do you seek to feel His presence and His peace? Then you must walk in truth; you must walk in the light; you must walk with the Savior. There is simply no other way.

If we do not radiate the light of Christ around us, the sense of the darkness that prevails in the world will increase.

MOTHER TERESA

Unchanging Laws

God's Law is more real and lasting than the stars in the sky and the ground at your feet. Long after stars burn out and earth wears out, God's Law will be alive and working.

MATTHEW 5:18 MSG

God's laws are eternal and unchanging: obedience leads to abundance and joy; disobedience leads to disaster. God has given us a guidebook for righteous living called the Holy Bible. If we trust God's Word and live by it, we are blessed. But, if we choose to ignore God's commandments, the results are as predictable as they are tragic.

Life is a series of decisions and choices. Each day, we make countless decisions that can bring us closer to God . . . or not. When we live according to God's commandments, we earn for ourselves the abundance and peace that He intends for our lives.

Do you seek God's peace and His blessings? Then obey Him. When you're faced with a difficult choice or a powerful temptation, seek God's counsel and trust the counsel He gives. Invite God into your heart and live according to His commandments. When you do, you will be blessed today, and tomorrow, and forever.

Including God in Your Plans

Commit your activities to the Lord and your plans will be achieved.

PROVERBS 16:3 HCSB

Would you like a formula for successful living that never fails? Here it is: Include God in every aspect of your life's journey, including the plans that you make and the steps that you take. But beware: as you make plans for the days and weeks ahead, you may become sidetracked by the demands of everyday living.

If you allow the world to establish your priorities, you will eventually become discouraged, or disappointed, or both. But if you genuinely seek God's will for every important decision that you make, your loving Heavenly Father will guide your steps and enrich your life. So as you plan your work, remember that every good plan should start with God, including yours.

God has plans—not problems—for our lives. Before she died in the concentration camp in Ravensbruck, my sister Betsie said to me, "Corrie, your whole life has been a training for the work you are doing here in prison—and for the work you will do afterward."

CORRIE TEN BOOM

Pray About Your Plans

Your Father knows exactly what you need even before you ask him!

Your search to discover God's unfolding plan for your life is not a destination to be reached; it is a path to be traveled, a journey that unfolds every day of your life. And, that's exactly how often you should seek direction from your Creator: one day at a time, each day followed by the next, without exception.

Daily prayer and meditation is a matter of will and habit. You must willingly organize your time by carving out quiet moments with God, and you must form the habit of daily worship. When you do, you'll discover that no time is more precious than the silent moments you spend with your Heavenly Father.

The quality of your spiritual life will be in direct proportion to the quality of your prayer life. Prayer changes things, and it changes you. Today, weave the power of prayer into the very fabric of your life. Don't limit your prayers to meals or to bedtime; pray constantly. God is listening; He wants to hear from you; and you most certainly need to hear from Him.

Your Questions, His Answers

Our God forever and ever . . . will guide us until death.

PSALM 48:14 NASB

When you have a question that you simply can't answer, whom do you ask? When you face a difficult decision, to whom do you turn for counsel? To friends? To mentors? To family members? Or do you turn first to the Ultimate source of wisdom? The answers to life's Big Questions start with God and with the teachings of His Holy Word.

God's wisdom stands forever. God's Word is a light for every generation. Make it your light as well. Use the Bible as a compass for the next stage of your life's journey. Use it as the yardstick by which your behavior is measured. And as you carefully consult the pages of God's Word, prayerfully ask Him to reveal the wisdom that you need. When you take your concerns to God, He will not turn you away; He will, instead, offer answers that are tested and true. Your job is to ask, to listen, and to trust.

We are finding we don't have such a gnawing need to know the answers when we know the Answer.

GLORIA GAITHER

Using Your Gifts to Serve

Each of you should look not only to your own interests, but also to the interest of others.

PHILIPPIANS 2:4 NIV

Jesus teaches that the most esteemed men and women are not the leaders of society or the captains of industry. To the contrary, Jesus teaches that the greatest among us are those who choose to minister and to serve.

Today, you may feel the temptation to build yourself up in the eyes of your neighbors. Resist that temptation. Instead, serve your neighbors quietly and without fanfare. Find a need and fill it . . . humbly. Lend a helping hand and share a word of kindness . . . anonymously.

Today, take the time to minister to those in need. Then, when you have done your best to serve your neighbors and to serve your God, you can rest comfortably knowing that in the eyes of God you have achieved greatness. And God's eyes, after all, are the only ones that really count.

We have to serve God in His way, not in ours.

ST. TERESA OF AVILA

Stillness

Be still, and know that I am God . . . .

Psalm 46:10 KJV

Are you so busy that you rush through the day with scarcely a single moment for quiet contemplation and prayer? If so, it's time to reorder your priorities.

We live in a noisy world, a world filled with distractions, frustrations, and complications. But if we allow the distractions of a clamorous world to separate us from God's peace, we do ourselves a profound disservice. If we are to maintain righteous minds and compassionate hearts, we must take time each day for prayer and for meditation. We must make ourselves still in the presence of our Creator. We must quiet our minds and our hearts so that we might sense God's will, God's love, and God's Son.

Has the busy pace of life robbed you of the peace that might otherwise be yours through Jesus Christ? Nothing is more important than the time you spend with your Savior. So be still and claim the inner peace that is your spiritual birthright: the peace of Jesus Christ. It is offered freely; it has been paid for in full; it is yours for the asking. So ask. And then share.

Too Busy to Give Thanks?

Enter into His gates with thanksgiving, and into His courts with praise. Be thankful to Him, and bless His name. For the Lord is good; His mercy is everlasting, and His truth endures to all generations.

PSALM 100:4-5 NKJV

Life has a way of constantly coming at us. Days, hours, and moments are filled with urgent demands requiring our immediate attention.

When the demands of life leave us rushing from place to place with scarcely a moment to spare, we may fail to pause and thank our Creator for His gifts. But, whenever we neglect to give proper thanks to the Father, we suffer because of our misplaced priorities.

Today, make a special effort to give thanks to the Creator for His blessings. His love for you is eternal, as are His gifts. And it's never too soon—or too late—to offer Him thanks.

Is it any wonder . . . that your heart goes up to God in glad thanksgiving that he has so trusted you as to commit to your hands this darkness?

LOTTIE MOON

Knowing the Truth

Buy—and do not sell—truth, wisdom, instruction, and
understanding.

PROVERBS 23:23 HCSB

The familiar words of John 8:32 remind us that "you shall know the truth, and the truth shall make you free" (NKJV). And St. Augustine had this advice: "Let everything perish! Dismiss these empty vanities! And let us take up the search for the truth."

God is vitally concerned with truth. His Word teaches the truth; His Spirit reveals the truth; His Son leads us to the truth. When we open our hearts to God, and when we allow His Son to rule over our thoughts and our lives, God reveals Himself, and we come to understand the truth about ourselves and the Truth about God's gift of grace.

Are you seeking the truth and living by it? Hopefully so. When you do, you'll discover that the truth will indeed set you free, now and forever.

Only Jesus Christ is the truth for everyone who has ever been born into the human race, regardless of culture, age, nationality, generation, heritage, gender, color, or language.

ANNE GRAHAM LOTZ

God Has Work for You

Work hard, but not just to please your masters when they are watching. As slaves of Christ, do the will of God with all your heart. Work with enthusiasm, as though you were working for the Lord rather than for people.

EPHESIANS 6:6-7 NLT

God has work for you to do, but He won't make you do it. Since the days of Adam and Eve, God has allowed His children to make choices for themselves, and so it is with you. You've got choices to make . . . lots of them. If you choose wisely, you'll be rewarded; if you choose unwisely, you'll bear the consequences.

Whether you're in school or in the workplace, your success will depend, in large part, upon the quality and quantity of your work. God has created a world in which diligence is rewarded and sloth is not. So whatever you choose to do, do it with commitment, excitement, and vigor.

God did not create you for a life of mediocrity; He created you for far greater things. Reaching for greater things usually requires work and lots of it, which is perfectly fine with God. After all, He knows that you're up to the task, and He has big plans for you. Very big plans . . .

Where to Take Your Concerns

Do not worry about anything, but pray and ask God for everything you need, always giving thanks.

PHILIPPIANS 4:6 NCV

If you are like most women, it is simply a fact of life: from time to time, you worry. You worry about health, about finances, about safety, about relationships, about family, and about countless other challenges of life, some great and some small. Where is the best place to take your worries? Take them to God. Take your troubles to Him, and your fears, and your sorrows.

Barbara Johnson correctly observed, "Worry is the senseless process of cluttering up tomorrow's opportunities with leftover problems from today." So if you'd like to make the most out of this day (and every one hereafter), turn your worries over to a Power greater than yourself . . . and spend your valuable time and energy solving the problems you can fix . . . while trusting God to do the rest.

Remember always that there are two things which are more utterly incompatible even than oil and water, and these two are trust and worry.

HANNAH WHITALL SMITH

Spiritual Traps

Why are you cast down, O my soul? And why are you disquieted within me? Hope in God; for I shall yet praise Him, the help of my countenance and my God.

PSALM 42:11 NKJV

Pessimism and Christianity don't mix. Why? Because Christians have every reason to be optimistic about life here on earth and life eternal.

Sometimes, despite our trust in God, we may fall into the spiritual traps of worry, frustration, anxiety, or sheer exhaustion, and our hearts become heavy. What's needed is plenty of rest, a large dose of perspective, and God's healing touch, but not necessarily in that order.

Today, make this promise to yourself and keep it: vow to be a hope-filled Christian. Think optimistically about your life, your profession, and your future. Trust your hopes, not your fears. Take time to celebrate God's glorious creation. And then, when you've filled your heart with hope and gladness, share your optimism with others. They'll be better for it, and so will you. But not necessarily in that order.

God's Policy

Lying lips are an abomination to the Lord, but those who deal truthfully are His delight.

PROVERBS 12:22 NKJV

From the time we are children, we are taught that honesty is the best policy, but sometimes, it is so hard to be honest and so easy to be less than honest. So, we convince ourselves that it's alright to tell "little white lies." But there's a problem: Little white lies tend to grow up, and when they do, they cause havoc and pain in our lives.

For Christian believers, the issue of honesty is not a topic for debate. Honesty is not just the best policy, it is God's policy, pure and simple. And if we are to be servants worthy of our Savior, Jesus Christ, we avoid all lies, white or otherwise.

Sometime soon, perhaps even today, you will be tempted to sow the seeds of deception, perhaps in the form of a "harmless" white lie. Resist that temptation. Truth is God's way, and a lie—of whatever color—is not.

Much guilt arises in the life of the believer from practicing the chameleon life of environmental adaptation.

BETH MOORE

Acceptance and Peace

Come to terms with God and be at peace; in this way good will come to you.

JOB 22:21 HCSB

All of us experience adversity and pain. As human beings with limited understanding, we can never fully understand the will of our Father in heaven. But as believers in a benevolent God, we must always trust His providence.

When Jesus went to the Mount of Olives, as described in Luke 22, He poured out His heart to God. Jesus knew of the agony that He was destined to endure, but He also knew that God's will must be done. We, like our Savior, face trials that bring fear and trembling to the very depths of our souls, but like Christ, we, too, must ultimately seek God's will, not our own.

Are you embittered by a personal tragedy that you did not deserve and cannot understand? If so, it's time to make peace with life. It's time to forgive others, and, if necessary, to forgive yourself. It's time to accept the unchangeable past, to embrace the priceless present, and to have faith in the promise of tomorrow. It's time to trust God completely. And it's time to reclaim the peace—His peace—that can and should be yours.

Restoring Your Hope

*Until now you have not asked for anything in my name.
Ask and you will receive, so that your joy will be the fullest
possible joy.*

JOHN 16:24 NCV

Have you fervently asked God to restore your hope for tomorrow? Have you asked Him for guidance and strength? If so, then you're continually inviting your Creator to reveal Himself in a variety of ways. As a follower of Christ, you must do no less.

Jesus made it clear to His disciples: they should petition God to meet their needs. So should we. Genuine, heartfelt prayer produces powerful changes in us and in our world. When we lift our hearts to God, we open ourselves to a never-ending source of divine wisdom and infinite love.

Do you have questions about your future that you simply can't answer? Do you have needs that you simply can't meet by yourself? Do you sincerely seek to know God's purpose for your life? If so, ask Him for direction, for protection, and for strength—and then keep asking Him every day that you live. Whatever your need, no matter how great or small, pray about it and never lose hope. God is not just near; He is here, and He's perfectly capable of answering your prayers.

Too Busy

Don't burn out; keep yourselves fueled and aflame. Be alert servants of the Master, cheerfully expectant. Don't quit in hard times; pray all the harder.

ROMANS 12:11-12 MSG

Has the busy pace of life robbed you of the peace that might otherwise be yours through Jesus Christ? If so, you are simply too busy for your own good. Through His Son Jesus, God offers you a peace that passes human understanding, but He won't force His peace upon you; in order to experience it, you must slow down long enough to sense His presence and His love.

Today, as a gift to yourself, to your family, and to the world, slow down and claim the inner peace that is your spiritual birthright: the peace of Jesus Christ. It is offered freely; it has been paid for in full; it is yours for the asking. So ask. And then share.

To do too much is as dangerous as to do nothing at all. Both modes prevent us from savoring our moments. One causes me to rush right past the best of life without recognizing or basking in it, and the other finds me sitting quietly as life rushes past me.

PATSY CLAIRMONT

Worshipping the Christ Child

For there is born to you this day in the city of David a Savior, who is Christ the Lord. And this will be the sign to you: You will find a Babe wrapped in swaddling cloths, lying in a manger.

LUKE 2:11-12 NKJV

God sent His Son to transform the world and to save it. The Christ Child was born in the most humble of circumstances: in a nondescript village, to parents of simple means, far from the seats of earthly power.

God sent His Son, not as a conqueror or a king, but as an innocent babe. Jesus came, not to be served, but to serve. Jesus did not preach a message of retribution or revenge; He spoke words of compassion and forgiveness. We must do our best to imitate Him.

In the second chapter of Luke, we read about shepherds who were tending their flocks on the night Christ was born. May we, like those shepherds of old, leave our fields—wherever they may be—and pause to worship God's priceless gift: His only begotten Son.

Our temporal gifts, go under a tree. Our eternal gift, hung from a tree.

ANONYMOUS

Critics Beware

So let's agree to use all our energy in getting along with each other. Help others with encouraging words; don't drag them down by finding fault.

ROMANS 14:19-20 MSG

From experience, we know that it is easier to criticize than to correct. And we know that it is easier to find faults than solutions. Yet the urge to criticize others remains a powerful temptation for most of us.

In the book of James, we are issued a clear warning: "Don't criticize one another, brothers" (4:11). Undoubtedly, James understood the paralyzing power of chronic negativity, and so should we.

Negativity is highly contagious: we give it to others who, in turn, give it back to us. This cycle can be broken by positive thoughts, heartfelt prayers, and encouraging words. As thoughtful servants of a loving God, we can use the transforming power of Christ's love to break the chains of negativity. And we should.

If I long to improve my brother, the first step toward doing so is to improve myself.

CHRISTINA ROSSETTI

Faith Above Feelings

The righteous will live by his faith.

HABAKKUK 2:4 NIV

Hebrews 10:38 teaches that we should live by faith. Yet sometimes, despite our best intentions, negative feelings can rob us of the peace and abundance that would otherwise be ours through Christ. When anger or anxiety separates us from the spiritual blessings that God has in store, we must rethink our priorities and renew our faith. And we must place faith above feelings. Human emotions are highly variable, decidedly unpredictable, and often unreliable. Our emotions are like the weather, only far more fickle. So we must learn to live by faith, not by the ups and downs of our own emotional roller coasters.

Sometime during this day, you will probably be gripped by a strong negative emotion. Distrust it. Reign it in. Test it. And turn it over to God. Your emotions will inevitably change; God will not. So trust Him completely as you watch your feelings slowly evaporate into thin air—which, of course, they will.

Emotions we have not poured out in the safe hands of God can turn into feelings of hopelessness and depression. God is safe.

BETH MOORE

We Are All Role Models

You should be an example to the believers in speech, in conduct, in love, in faith, in purity.

1 TIMOTHY 4:12 HCSB

Whether we like it or not, all of us are role models. Our friends and family members watch our actions and, as followers of Christ, we are obliged to act accordingly.

What kind of example are you? Are you the kind of woman whose life serves as a genuine example of righteousness? Are you a woman whose behavior serves as a positive role model for young people? Are you the kind of woman whose actions, day in and day out, are based upon kindness, faithfulness, and a love for the Lord? If so, you are not only blessed by God, you are also a powerful force for good in a world that desperately needs positive influences such as yours.

Corrie ten Boom advised, "Don't worry about what you do not understand. Worry about what you do understand in the Bible but do not live by." And that's sound advice because our families and friends are watching . . . and so, for that matter, is God.

Look Upward to Him

So God raised him to the highest place. God made his name greater than every other name so that every knee will bow to the name of Jesus—everyone in heaven, on earth, and under the earth. And everyone will confess that Jesus Christ is Lord and bring glory to God the Father.

PHILIPPIANS 2:9-11 NCV

Hannah Whitall Smith spoke to believers of every generation when she advised, "Keep your face upturned to Christ as the flowers do to the sun. Look, and your soul shall live and grow." That's powerful advice. When we turn our hearts to Jesus, we receive His blessings, His peace, and His grace.

Do you regularly take time each day to embrace Christ's love? Do you prayerfully ask God to lead you in the footsteps of His Son? And are you determined to obey God's Word even if the world encourages you to do otherwise? If so, you'll soon experience the peace and the power that flows freely from the Son of God.

The love life of the Christian is a crucial battleground. There, if nowhere else, it will be determined who is Lord: the world, the self, and the devil—or the Lord Christ.

ELISABETH ELLIOT

Taking Time to Enjoy

Until now you have asked for nothing in My name. Ask and you will receive, that your joy may be complete.

JOHN 16:24 HCSB

Are you a woman who takes time each day to really enjoy life? Hopefully so. After all, you are the recipient of a precious gift—the gift of life. And because God has seen fit to give you this gift, it is incumbent upon you to use it and to enjoy it. But sometimes, amid the inevitable pressures of everyday living, really enjoying life may seem almost impossible. It is not.

For most of us, fun is as much a function of attitude as it is a function of environment. So whether you're standing victorious atop one of life's mountains or trudging through one of life's valleys, enjoy yourself. You deserve to have fun today, and God wants you to have fun today . . . so what on earth are you waiting for?

Whence comes this idea that if what we are doing is fun, it can't be God's will? The God who made giraffes, a baby's fingernails, a puppy's tail, a crooknecked squash, the bobwhite's call, and a young girl's giggle, has a sense of humor. Make no mistake about that.

CATHERINE MARSHALL

Showers of Blessings

I will bless them and the places surrounding my hill. I will send down showers in season; there will be showers of blessings.

EZEKIEL 34:26 NIV

Do you know how richly you have been blessed? Well, God's gifts are actually too numerous to count, but you are wise to inventory as many blessings as you can, as often as you can.

Elisabeth Elliot noted, "It is always possible to be thankful for what is given rather than to complain about what is not given. One or the other becomes a habit of life." And Gloria Gaither observed, "God has promised that if we harvest well with the tools of thanksgiving, there will be seeds for planting in the spring."

Are you taking God's gifts for granted? If so, you are doing a disservice to your Creator and to yourself. And the best way to resolve that problem is to make this day (and every day) a time for celebration and praise. Starting now.

The Bible plainly teaches that if we will learn and act on the Word, God will bless our lives.

JOYCE MEYER

He Loves You

Therefore humble yourselves under the mighty hand of God, that He may exalt you at the proper time, casting all your anxiety on Him, because He cares for you.

1 PETER 5:6-7 NASB

When we worship God with faith and assurance, when we place Him at the absolute center of our lives, we invite His love into our hearts. In turn, we grow to love Him more deeply as we sense His love for us. St. Augustine wrote, "I love you, Lord, not doubtingly, but with absolute certainty. Your Word beat upon my heart until I fell in love with you, and now the universe and everything in it tells me to love you." Let us pray that we, too, will turn our hearts to our Heavenly Father, knowing with certainty that He loves us and that we love Him.

God is love, and God's love is perfect. When we open ourselves to His perfect love, we are touched by the Creator's hand, and we are transformed, not just for a day, but for all eternity.

Today, as you carve out quiet moments of thanksgiving and praise for your Heavenly Father, open yourself to His presence and to His love. He is here, waiting. His love is here, always. Accept it—now—and be blessed.

What Do You Expect?

I say to myself, "The Lord is mine, so I hope in him."

LAMENTATIONS 3:24 NCV

What do you expect from the day ahead? Are you expecting God to do wonderful things, or are you living beneath a cloud of apprehension and doubt? The familiar words of Psalm 118:24 remind us of a profound yet simple truth: "This is the day which the LORD hath made; we will rejoice and be glad in it" (KJV).

For Christian believers, every day begins and ends with God's Son and God's promises. When we accept Christ into our hearts, God promises us the opportunity for earthly peace and spiritual abundance. But more importantly, God promises us the priceless gift of eternal life.

As we face the inevitable challenges of life-here-on-earth, we must arm ourselves with the promises of God's Holy Word. When we do, we can expect the best, not only for the day ahead, but also for all eternity.

Claim all of God's promises in the Bible. Your sins, your worries, your life—you may cast them all on Him.

CORRIE TEN BOOM

God's Will for You

And this world is fading away, along with everything it craves. But if you do the will of God, you will live forever.

1 John 2:17 NLT

As human beings with limited understanding, we can never fully comprehend the will of God. But as believers in a benevolent God, we must always trust the will of our Heavenly Father.

Before His crucifixion, Jesus went to the Mount of Olives and poured out His heart to God (Luke 22). Jesus knew of the agony that He was destined to endure, but He also knew that God's will must be done. We, like our Savior, face trials that bring fear and trembling to the very depths of our souls, but like Christ, we, too, must ultimately seek God's will, not our own.

As this day unfolds, seek God's will for your own life and obey His Word. When you entrust your life to Him completely and without reservation, He will give you the strength to meet any challenge, the courage to face any trial, and the wisdom to live in His righteousness and in His peace.

Life isn't life without some divine decisions that our mortal minds simply cannot comprehend.

BETH MOORE

When We Lose Hope

Be of good courage, and He shall strengthen your heart, all you who hope in the Lord.

PSALM 31:24 NKJV

As every woman knows, hope is a perishable commodity. Despite God's promises, despite Christ's love, and despite our countless blessings, we frail human beings can still lose hope from time to time. When we do, we need the encouragement of Christian friends, the life-changing power of prayer, and the healing truth of God's Holy Word. If we find ourselves falling into the spiritual traps of worry and discouragement, we should seek the healing touch of Jesus and the encouraging words of fellow Christians. Even though this world can be a place of trials and struggles, God has promised us peace, joy, and eternal life if we give ourselves to Him.

Joy lifts our spirit above earth's sorrow, dancing in jubilation at the hope set before us.

SUSAN LENZKES

Hope is faith holding out its hand in the dark.

BARBARA JOHNSON

Where Wisdom Is Found

Only the Lord gives wisdom; he gives knowledge and understanding.

PROVERBS 2:6 NCV

If we are to grow as Christians and as women, we need both knowledge and wisdom. Knowledge is found in textbooks. Wisdom, on the other hand, is found in God's Holy Word and in the carefully-chosen words of loving parents, family members, and friends. Knowledge is an important building block in a well-lived life, and it pays rich dividends both personally and professionally. But, wisdom is even more important because it refashions not only the mind, but also the heart.

A big difference exists between a head full of knowledge and the words of God literally abiding in us.

BETH MOORE

It is never enough to know about spiritual things with your mind. Mental knowledge is not the same thing as truly understanding from the center of your being, which results from experiencing and doing.

ST. TERESA OF AVILA

The Miracle Worker

Is anything impossible for the Lord?

God is a miracle worker. Throughout history He has intervened in the course of human events in ways that cannot be explained by science or human rationale. And He's still doing so today.

God's miracles are not limited to special occasions, nor are they witnessed by a select few. God is crafting His wonders all around us: the miracle of the birth of a new baby; the miracle of a world renewing itself with every sunrise; the miracle of lives transformed by God's love and grace. Each day, God's handiwork is evident for all to see and experience.

Today, seize the opportunity to inspect God's hand at work. His miracles come in a variety of shapes and sizes, so keep your eyes and your heart open. Be watchful, and you'll soon be amazed.

I believe that God is in the miracle business—that his favorite way of working is to pick up where our human abilities and understandings leave off and then do something so wondrous and unexpected that there's no doubt who the God is around here.

EMILIE BARNES

Being Patient with God's Timing

I wait for the Lord; I wait, and put my hope in His word.
PSALM 130:5 HCSB

As individuals, as families, as businesses, and as a nation, we are impatient for the changes that we so earnestly desire. We want solutions to our problems, and we want them right now! But sometimes, life's greatest challenges defy easy solutions, so we must be patient.

Psalm 37:7 commands us to "Rest in the Lord, and wait patiently for Him" (NKJV). But for most of us, waiting quietly for God is difficult. Why? Because we are imperfect beings who seek solutions to our problems today, if not sooner. We seek to manage our lives according to our own timetables, not God's. To do so is a mistake. Instead of impatiently tapping our fingers, we should fold our fingers and pray. When we do, our Heavenly Father will reward us in His own miraculous way and in His own perfect time.

How do you wait upon the Lord? First you must learn to sit at His feet and take time to listen to His words.

KAY ARTHUR

Good Pressures, Bad Pressures

Do not be fooled: "Bad friends will ruin good habits."
1 CORINTHIANS 15:33 NCV

Our world is filled with pressures: some good, some bad. The pressures that we feel to behave responsibly are positive pressures. God places these pressures on our hearts, and He intends that we act accordingly. But we also face different pressures, ones that are definitely not from God.

Society seeks to mold us into more worldly beings; God seeks to mold us into new beings, more spiritual beings, beings that are most certainly not conformed to this world.

If we desire to lead responsible lives—and if we seek to please God—we must resist the pressures that society seeks to impose upon us. We must resist the temptation to do the "popular" thing, and we must insist, instead, upon doing the right thing. Period!

We, as God's people, are not only to stay far away from sin and sinners who would entice us, but we are to be so like our God that we mourn over sin.

KAY ARTHUR

Praising the Savior

At the name of Jesus every knee should bow, of those in heaven, and of those on earth, and of those under the earth, and that every tongue should confess that Jesus Christ is Lord, to the glory of God the Father.

PHILIPPIANS 2:10-11 NKJV

The words by Fanny Crosby are familiar: "This is my story, this is my song, praising my Savior, all the day long." As believers who have been saved by the blood of a risen Christ, we must do exactly as the song instructs: We must praise our Savior time and time again throughout the day. Worship and praise should be a part of everything we do. Otherwise, we quickly lose perspective as we fall prey to the demands of everyday life.

Do you sincerely desire to be a worthy servant of the One who has given you eternal love and eternal life? Then praise Him for who He is and for what He has done for you. And don't just praise Him on Sunday morning. Praise Him all day long, every day, for as long as you live . . . and then for all eternity.

Praise Him! Praise Him! Tell of His excellent greatness. Praise Him! Praise Him! Ever in joyful song!

FANNY CROSBY

What Now, Lord?

For we are His making, created in Christ Jesus for good works, which God prepared ahead of time so that we should walk in them.

EPHESIANS 2:10 HCSB

God has things He wants you to do and places He wants you to go. The most important decision of your life is, of course, your commitment to accept Jesus as your personal Lord and Savior. And, once your eternal destiny is secured, you will undoubtedly ask yourself the question "What now, Lord?" If you earnestly seek God's will for your life, you will find it . . . in time.

As you prayerfully consider God's path for your life, you should study His Word and be ever watchful for His signs. You should associate with fellow believers who will encourage your spiritual growth, and you should listen to that inner voice that speaks to you in the quiet moments of your daily devotionals.

As you continually seek God's purpose for your life, be patient: your Heavenly Father may not always reveal Himself as quickly as you would like. But rest assured: God is here, and He intends to use you in wonderful, unexpected ways. He desires to lead you along a path of His choosing. Your challenge is to watch, to listen... and to follow.

His Plan for You

For I am not ashamed of this Good News about Christ. It is the power of God at work, saving everyone who believes.

ROMANS 1:16 NLT

How marvelous it is that God became a man and walked among us. Had He not chosen to do so, we might feel removed from a distant Creator. But ours is not a distant God. Ours is a God who understands—far better than we ever could—the essence of what it means to be human.

God understands our hopes, our fears, and our temptations. He understands what it means to be angry and what it costs to forgive. He knows the heart, the conscience, and the soul of every person who has ever lived, including you. And God has a plan of salvation that is intended for you. Accept it. Accept God's gift through the person of His Son Christ Jesus, and then rest assured: God walked among us so that you might have eternal life; amazing though it may seem, He did it for you.

Though the details may differ from story to story, we are all sinners—saved only by the wonderful grace of God.

GLORIA GAITHER

A Word Aptly Spoken

Kind words are like honey—sweet to the soul and healthy for the body.

PROVERBS 16:24 NLT

In the Book of Proverbs, we read that, "A word aptly spoken is like apples of gold in settings of silver" (25:11 NIV). This verse reminds us that the words we speak can and should be beautiful offerings to those who hear them.

All of us have the power to enrich the lives of others. Sometimes, when we feel uplifted and secure, it is easy to speak words of encouragement and hope. Other times, when we are discouraged or tired, we can scarcely summon the energy to uplift ourselves, much less anyone else. But, as loving Christians, our obligation is clear: we must always measure our words carefully as we use them to benefit our neighbors and to glorify our Father in heaven.

God intends that we speak words of kindness, wisdom, and truth, no matter our circumstances, no matter our emotions. When we do, we share a priceless gift with the world, and we give glory to the One who gave His life for us. As believers, we must do no less.

Beyond the Temptations

Then Jesus told him, "Go away, Satan! For it is written: You must worship the Lord your God, and you must serve Him only."

MATTHEW 4:10 HCSB

After fasting forty days and nights in the desert, Jesus was tempted by Satan. Christ used Scripture to rebuke the devil (Matthew 4: 1-11). We must do likewise. The Holy Bible provides us with a perfect blueprint for righteous living. If we consult that blueprint daily and follow it carefully, we build our lives according to God's plan.

We live in a world that is brimming with opportunities to stray from God's will. Ours is a society filled with temptations, a place where it is all too easy to disobey God. We, like our Savior, must guard ourselves against these temptations. We do so, in part, through prayer and through a careful reading of God's Word.

The battle against Satan is ongoing. Be vigilant, and call upon your Heavenly Father to protect you. When you petition Him with a sincere heart, God will be your shield, now and forever.

Expecting the Best

Let us hold fast the confession of our hope without wavering, for He who promised is faithful.

HEBREWS 10:23 NKJV

What do you expect from the day ahead? Are you expecting God to do wonderful things, or are you living beneath a cloud of apprehension and doubt? The familiar words of Psalm 118:24 remind us of a profound yet simple truth: "This is the day which the LORD hath made; we will rejoice and be glad in it" (KJV).

For Christian believers, every day begins and ends with God and His Son. Christ came to this earth to give us abundant life and eternal salvation. We give thanks to our Maker when we treasure each day and use it to the fullest. Today, let us give thanks for the gift of life and for the One who created it. And then, let's use this day—a precious gift from the Father above—to serve our Savior and to share His Good News with all who cross our paths.

The whole essence of the spiritual life consists in recognizing the designs of God for us at the present moment.

ELISABETH ELLIOT

The Tapestry of Life

Let not your heart be troubled; you believe in God, believe also in Me. In My Father's house are many mansions; if it were not so, I would have told you. I go to prepare a place for you. And if I go and prepare a place for you, I will come again and receive you to Myself; that where I am, there you may be also.

JOHN 14:1-3 NKJV

Life is a tapestry of good days and difficult days, with good days predominating. During the good days, we are tempted to take our blessings for granted (a temptation that we must resist with all our might). But, during life's difficult days, we discover precisely what we're made of. And more importantly, we discover what our faith is made of.

Has your faith been put to the test yet? If so, then you know that with God's help, you can endure life's darker days. But if you have not yet faced the inevitable trials and tragedies of life-here-on-earth, don't worry: you will. And when your faith is put to the test, rest assured that God is perfectly willing—and always ready—to give you strength for the struggle.

God's Guidebook

All Scripture is given by inspiration of God, and is profitable for doctrine, for reproof, for correction, for instruction in righteousness, that the man of God may be complete, thoroughly equipped for every good work.

2 TIMOTHY 3:16-17 NKJV

God has given us a guidebook for righteous living called the Holy Bible. It contains thorough instructions which, if followed, lead to fulfillment, righteousness, and salvation. But, if we choose to ignore God's commandments, the results are as predictable as they are tragic.

God has given us the Bible for the purpose of knowing His promises, His power, His commandments, His wisdom, His love, and His Son. As we study God's teachings and apply them to our lives, we live by the Word that shall never pass away.

Today, let us follow God's commandments, and let us conduct our lives in such a way that we might be shining examples to our students, to our families, and, most importantly, to those who have not yet found Christ.

Why Me?

I have heard your prayer, I have seen your tears; surely I will heal you.

2 KINGS 20:5 NKJV

When life unfolds according to our wishes, or when we experience unexpected good fortune, we find it easy to praise God's plan. That's when we greet change with open arms. But sometimes the changes that we must endure are painful. When we struggle through the difficult days of life, as we must from time to time, we may ask ourselves, "Why me?" The answer, of course, is that God knows, but He isn't telling . . . yet.

Have you endured a difficult transition that has left your head spinning or your heart broken? If so, you have a clear choice to make: either you can cry and complain, or you can trust God and get busy fixing what's broken. The former is a formula for disaster; the latter is a formula for a well-lived life.

If God has you in the palm of his hand and your real life is secure in him, then you can venture forth—into the places and relationships, the challenges, the very heart of the storm—and you will be safe there.

PAULA RINEHART

Obedience and Contentment

*Praise the Lord! Happy are those who respect the Lord,
who want what he commands.*

PSALM 112:1 NCV

When we conduct ourselves in ways that are opposed to God's commandments, we rob ourselves of God's peace. When we fall prey to the temptations and distractions of our irreverent age, we rob ourselves of God's blessings. When we become preoccupied with material possessions or personal status, we forfeit the contentment that is rightfully ours in Christ.

Where can we find the kind of contentment that Paul describes in Philippians 4:11? Is it a result of wealth, or power, or fame? Hardly. Genuine contentment is a gift from God to those who follow His commandments and accept His Son. It is a gift that must be discovered and rediscovered throughout life. It is a gift that we claim when we allow Christ to dwell at the center of our lives.

When we do what is right, we have contentment, peace, and happiness.

BEVERLY LAHAYE

God Rewards Discipline

Apply your heart to discipline And your ears to words of knowledge.

PROVERBS 23:12 NASB

God's Word reminds us again and again that our Creator expects us to lead disciplined lives. God doesn't reward laziness, misbehavior, or apathy. To the contrary, He expects believers to behave with dignity and discipline.

We live in a world in which leisure is glorified and indifference is often glamorized. But God has other plans. He did not create us for lives of mediocrity; He created us for far greater things.

Life's greatest rewards seldom fall into our laps; to the contrary, our greatest accomplishments usually require lots of work, which is perfectly fine with God. After all, He knows that we're up to the task, and He has big plans for us; may we, as disciplined believers, always be worthy of those plans.

God "longs to be gracious" to us (Isaiah 30:18), and He carries out His judgment against our sin with holy sorrow, intending His discipline to be a vehicle of mercy toward us.

NANCY GROOM

All the Energy You Need

Whatever you do, do it enthusiastically, as something done for the Lord and not for men.

COLOSSIANS 3:23 HCSB

Are you fired with enthusiasm for Christ? If so, congratulations, and keep up the good work! But, if your spiritual batteries are running low, then perhaps you're spending too much energy working for yourself and not enough energy working for God.

We mortals are at our best when we give. Some of us try desperately to hold on to ourselves, to live for ourselves. But giving is our nature, and we are never fully at peace unless we are faithfully living in accordance with God's will for our lives. God's instructions are clear. As believers, we are to be generous, enthusiastic stewards of the talents and energies that God has bestowed upon us.

Are you an energized Christian? You should be. But if you're not, you must seek strength and renewal from the one source that will never fail: that source, of course, is your Heavenly Father. And rest assured—when you sincerely petition Him, He will give you all the strength you need to live victoriously for Him.

God Protects

I know whom I have believed, and am convinced that he is able to guard what I have entrusted to him for that day.

2 TIMOTHY 1:12 NIV

God is willing to protect us. We, in turn, must open ourselves to His protection and His love. This point is illustrated by the familiar story found in the 4th chapter of Mark: When a terrible storm rose quickly on the Sea of Galilee, the disciples were afraid. Although they had witnessed many miracles, the disciples feared for their lives, so they turned to Jesus, and He calmed the waters and the wind.

Sometimes, we, like the disciples, feel threatened by the storms of life. And when we are fearful, we, too, can turn to Christ for comfort and for courage. The next time you find yourself facing a fear-provoking situation, remember that the One who calmed the wind and the waves is also your personal Savior. Then ask yourself which is stronger: your faith or your fear. The answer, friends, should be obvious: Whatever your challenge, God can handle it. Let Him.

Forgiveness Is a Choice

Above all, love each other deeply, because love covers a multitude of sins.

1 PETER 4:8 NIV

Forgiveness is a choice. We can either choose to forgive those who have injured us, or not. When we obey God by offering forgiveness to His children, we are blessed. But when we allow bitterness and resentment to poison our hearts, we are tortured by our own shortsightedness.

Do you harbor resentment against anyone? If so, you are faced with an important decision: whether or not to forgive the person who has hurt you. God's instructions are clear: He commands you to forgive. God doesn't suggest that you forgive or request that you forgive; He commands it. Period.

To forgive or not to forgive: that is the question. The answer should be obvious. The time to forgive is now because tomorrow may be too late . . . for you.

Forgiveness is not an emotion. Forgiveness is an act of the will, and the will can function regardless of the temperature of the heart.

CORRIE TEN BOOM

God Can Handle It

God—His way is perfect; the word of the Lord is pure. He is a shield to all who take refuge in Him.

PSALM 18:30 HCSB

In 1967, a diving accident left Joni Eareckson Tada a quadraplegic. But she didn't give up. Unable to use her hands, she taught herself to paint fine art by holding a brush between her teeth. Then, the determined Mrs. Tada began writing. To date, she's completed over thirty books, and her ministry, Joni and Friends, touches the lives of millions.

Jesus said, "In this world you will have trouble. But take heart! I have overcome the world." So the next time you face a difficult day or an unexpected challenge, remember Joni's journey. If she could meet her challenges, so can you. So take heart, trust, and remember that no problem is too big for God.

When considering the size of your problems, there are two categories that you should never worry about: the problems that are small enough for you to handle, and the ones that aren't too big for God to handle.

MARIE T. FREEMAN

His Grace Is Not Earned

For by grace you are saved through faith, and this is not from yourselves; it is God's gift—not from works, so that no one can boast.

EPHESIANS 2:8-9 HCSB

God's grace is not earned . . . thank goodness! To earn God's love and His gift of eternal life would be far beyond the abilities of even the most righteous man or woman. Thankfully, grace is not an earthly reward for righteous behavior; it is a blessed spiritual gift which can be accepted by believers who dedicate themselves to God through Christ. When we accept Christ into our hearts, we are saved by His grace.

The familiar words of Ephesians 2:8 make God's promise perfectly clear: It is by grace we have been saved, through faith. We are saved not because of our good deeds but because of our faith in Christ.

Let us praise the Creator for His priceless gift, and let us share the Good News with all who cross our paths. We return our Father's love by accepting His grace and by sharing His message and His love. When we do, we are eternally blessed . . . and the Father smiles.

A Grand Plan

I will instruct you and teach you in the way you should go;
I will guide you with My eye.

PSALM 32:8 NKJV

God has plans for your life that are far grander than you can imagine. But He won't force you to follow His will; to the contrary, He has given you free will, the ability to make choices and decisions on your own. The most important decision of your life is, of course, your commitment to accept Jesus Christ as your personal Lord and Savior. And once your eternal destiny is secured, you will undoubtedly ask yourself "What now, Lord?" If you earnestly seek God's will for your life, you will find it . . . in time.

Sometimes, God's plans are crystal clear, but other times, He may lead you through the wilderness before He delivers you to the Promised Land. So be patient, keep praying, and keep seeking His will for your life. When you do, you'll be amazed at the marvelous things that an all-powerful, all-knowing God can do.

God has no problems, only plans. There is never panic in heaven.

CORRIE TEN BOOM

Guard Your Heart

Guard your heart above all else, for it is the source of life.
PROVERBS 4:23 HCSB

You are near and dear to God. He loves you more than you can imagine, and He wants the very best for you. And one more thing: God wants you to guard your heart.

Every day, you are faced with choices . . . lots of them. You can do the right thing, or not. You can tell the truth, or not. You can be kind, and generous, and obedient. Or not.

Your mind and your heart will usually tell you the right thing to do. And if you listen to your parents and grandparents, they will help you, too, by teaching you God's rules. Then, you will learn that doing the right thing is always better than doing the wrong thing. And, by obeying God's rules, you will guard your heart by giving it to His Son Jesus.

Today, the world will offer you countless opportunities to let down your guard and, by doing so, let the devil do his worst. Be watchful and obedient. Guard your heart by giving it to your Heavenly Father; it is safe with Him.

Sharing the Joy

Let the hearts of those who seek the Lord rejoice. Look to the Lord and his strength; seek his face always.

1 CHRONICLES 16:10-11 NIV

God's intends that His joy should become our joy. He intends that we, His children, should share His love, His joy, and His peace. Yet sometimes, amid the inevitable hustle and bustle of life-here-on-earth, we don't feel much like sharing. So we forfeit—albeit temporarily—God's joy as we wrestle with the challenges of everyday life.

If, today, your heart is heavy, open the door of your soul to your Heavenly Father. When you do, He will renew your spirit. And, if you already have the joy of Christ in your heart, share it freely. When you discover ways to make your joy become their joy, you will have discovered a wonderful way to say, "I love you" to your family, to your friends, and, most especially, to your God.

Our obedience does not make God any bigger or better than He already is. Anything God commands of us is so that our joy may be full—the joy of seeing His glory revealed to us and in us!

BETH MOORE

Embracing God's Love

We love him, because he first loved us.

1 JOHN 4:19 KJV

As a woman, you know the profound love that you hold in your heart for your own family and friends. As a child of God, you can only imagine the infinite love that your Heavenly Father holds for you.

God made you in His own image and gave you salvation through the person of His Son Jesus Christ. And now, precisely because you are a wondrous creation treasured by God, a question presents itself: What will you do in response to the Creator's love? Will you ignore it or embrace it? Will you return it or neglect it? That decision, of course, is yours and yours alone.

When you embrace God's love, your life's purpose is forever changed. When you embrace God's love, you feel differently about yourself, your neighbors, your family, and your world. More importantly, you share God's message—and His love—with others.

Your Heavenly Father—a God of infinite love and mercy—is waiting to embrace you with open arms. Accept His love today and forever.

Obedience in Action

Obey God and be at peace with him; this is the way to happiness.

JOB 22:21 NCV

Obedience to God is determined, not by words, but by deeds. Talking about righteousness is easy; living righteously is far more difficult, especially in today's temptation-filled world.

Since God created Adam and Eve, we human beings have been rebelling against our Creator. Why? Because we are unwilling to trust God's Word, and we are unwilling to follow His commandments. God has given us a guidebook for righteous living called the Holy Bible. It contains thorough instructions which, if followed, lead to fulfillment, righteousness and salvation. But, if we choose to ignore God's commandments, the results are as predictable as they are tragic.

Unless we are willing to abide by God's laws, all of our righteous proclamations ring hollow. How can we best proclaim our love for the Lord? By obeying Him. And, for further instructions, read the manual.

Whose Expectations?

The person who knows my commandments and keeps them, that's who loves me. And the person who loves me will be loved by my Father, and I will love him and make myself plain to him.

JOHN 14:21 MSG

Here's a quick quiz: Whose expectations are you trying to meet? A. Your friends' expectations B. Society's expectations C. God's expectations

If you're a Christian, the correct answer is C., but if you're overly concerned with either A. or B., you're not alone. Plenty of women invest too much energy trying to meet society's expectations and too little energy trying to please God. It's a common behavior, but it's also a very big mistake.

A better strategy, of course, is to try to please God first. To do so, you must prioritize your day according to God's commandments, and you must seek His will and His wisdom in all matters. Then, you can face each day with the assurance that the same God who created our universe out of nothingness will help you place first things first in your own life.

The Power of Prayer

Don't worry about anything, but in everything, through prayer and petition with thanksgiving, let your requests be made known to God.

PHILIPPIANS 4:6 HCSB

"The power of prayer": these words are so familiar, yet sometimes we forget what they mean. Prayer is a powerful tool for communicating with our Creator; it is an opportunity to commune with the Giver of all things good. Prayer helps us find strength for today and hope for the future. Prayer is not a thing to be taken lightly or to be used infrequently.

Is prayer an integral part of your daily life, or is it a hit-or-miss habit? Do you "pray without ceasing," or is your prayer life an afterthought?

The quality of your spiritual life will be in direct proportion to the quality of your prayer life. Prayer changes things, and it changes you. Today, instead of worrying about your next decision, ask God to lead the way. Don't limit your prayers to meals or to bedtime. Pray constantly about things great and small. God is listening, and He wants to hear from you now.

Getting Past the Regrets

And don't be wishing you were someplace else or with someone else. Where you are right now is God's place for you. Live and obey and love and believe right there.

1 CORINTHIANS 7:17 MSG

Bitterness can destroy you if you let it . . . so don't let it! If you are caught up in intense feelings of anger or regret, you know all too well the destructive power of these emotions. How can you rid yourself of these feelings? First, you must prayerfully ask God to free you from these feelings. Then, you must learn to catch yourself whenever thoughts of bitterness begin to attack you. Your challenge is this: You must learn to resist negative thoughts before they hijack your emotions.

Each of us has something broken in our lives: a broken promise, a broken dream, a broken marriage, a broken heart . . . and we must decide how we're going to deal with our brokenness. We can wallow in self-pity or regret, accomplishing nothing and having no fun or joy in our circumstances; or we can determine with our will to take a few risks, get out of our comfort zone, and see what God will do to bring unexpected delight in our time of need.

LUCI SWINDOLL

Finding Purpose Through Service

So prepare your minds for service and have self-control.
1 PETER 1:13 NCV

The teachings of Jesus are clear: We achieve greatness through service to others. But, as weak human beings, we sometimes fall short as we seek to puff ourselves up and glorify our own accomplishments. Jesus commands otherwise. He teaches us that the most esteemed men and women are not the self-congratulatory leaders of society but are instead the humblest of servants.

Today, you may feel the temptation to build yourself up in the eyes of your neighbors. Resist that temptation. Instead, serve your neighbors quietly and without fanfare. Find a need and fill it . . . humbly. Lend a helping hand and share a word of kindness . . . anonymously, for this is God's way.

As a humble servant, you will glorify yourself not before men, but before God, and that's what God intends. After all, earthly glory is fleeting: here today and all too soon gone. But, heavenly glory endures throughout eternity. So, the choice is yours: Either you can lift yourself up here on earth and be humbled in heaven, or vice versa. Choose vice versa.

The Source of Strength

Have you not known? Have you not heard? The everlasting God, the Lord, the Creator of the ends of the earth, neither faints nor is weary. His understanding is unsearchable. He gives power to the weak, and to those who have no might He increases strength.

ISAIAH 40:28-29 NKJV

God is a never-ending source of strength and courage if we call upon Him. When we are weary, He gives us strength. When we see no hope, God reminds us of His promises. When we grieve, God wipes away our tears.

Do you feel overwhelmed by today's responsibilities? Do you feel pressured by the ever-increasing demands of 21st-century life? Then turn your concerns and your prayers over to God. He knows your needs, and He has promised to meet those needs. Whatever your circumstances, God will protect you and care for you . . . if you let Him. Invite Him into your heart and allow Him to renew your spirits. When you trust Him and Him alone, He will never fail you.

We should talk to each other, but it's when we talk together with God that we are fully strengthened.

ANNIE CHAPMAN

Always Blessed

Surely the righteous shall give thanks to Your name; the upright shall dwell in Your presence.

PSALM 140:13 NKJV

As believing Christians, we are blessed beyond measure. God sent His only Son to die for our sins. And, God has given us the priceless gifts of eternal love and eternal life. We, in turn, are instructed to approach our Heavenly Father with reverence and thanksgiving. But, as busy women caught up in the inevitable demands of everyday life, we sometimes fail to pause and thank our Creator for the countless blessings He has bestowed upon us. When we slow down and express our gratitude to the One who made us, we enrich our own lives and the lives of those around us. Thanksgiving should become a habit, a regular part of our daily routines. Yes, God has blessed us beyond measure, and we owe Him everything, including our eternal praise.

Gratitude unlocks the fullness of life. It turns what we have into enough, and more. It turns denial into acceptance, chaos to order, confusion to clarity. It can turn a meal into a feast, a house into a home, a stranger into a friend. Gratitude makes sense of our past, brings peace for today, and creates a vision for tomorrow.

MELODY BEATTIE

Being Understood

Dear friends, if God loved us in this way, we also must love one another.

1 JOHN 4:11 HCSB

What a blessing it is when our friends and loved ones genuinely seek to understand who we are and what we think. Just as we seek to be understood by others, so, too, should we seek to understand the hopes and dreams of our family members and friends.

We live in a busy world, a place where it is all too easy to overlook the needs of others, but God's Word instructs us to do otherwise. In the Gospel of Matthew, Jesus declares, "In everything, therefore, treat people the same way you want them to treat you, for this is the Law and the Prophets" (Matthew 7:12 NASB).

Today, as you consider all the things that Christ has done in your life, honor Him by being a little kinder than necessary. Honor Christ by slowing down long enough to notice the trials and tribulations of your neighbors. Honor Christ by giving the gift of understanding to friends and to family members alike. As a believer who has been eternally blessed by a loving Savior, you should do no less.

The Rewards of Work

The plans of the diligent lead surely to plenty.

PROVERBS 21:5 NKJV

How does God intend for us to work? Does He intend for us to work diligently or does He, instead, reward mediocrity? The answer is obvious. God has created a world in which hard work is rewarded and sloppy work is not. Yet sometimes, we may seek ease over excellence, or we may be tempted to take shortcuts when God intends that we walk the straight and narrow path.

Today, heed God's Word by doing good work. Wherever you find yourself, whatever your job description, do your work, and do it with all your heart. When you do, you will most certainly win the recognition of your peers. But more importantly, God will bless your efforts and use you in ways that only He can understand. So do your work with focus and dedication. And leave the rest up to God.

The "product" is a better indication of my relationship to God than the "profession."

ANONYMOUS

Part of the Plan

I rejoiced with those who said to me, "Let us go to the house of the Lord."

PSALM 122:1 HCSB

God has a wonderful plan for your life, and an important part of that plan includes worship. We should never deceive ourselves: every life is based upon some form of worship. The question is not whether we worship, but what we worship.

Some of us choose to worship God. The result is a plentiful harvest of joy, peace, and abundance. Others distance themselves from God by foolishly worshiping earthly possessions and personal gratification. To do so is a mistake of profound proportions.

Have you accepted the grace of God's only begotten Son? Then worship Him. Worship Him today and every day. Worship Him with sincerity and thanksgiving. Write His name on your heart and rest assured that He, too, has written your name on His.

To worship Him in truth means to worship Him honestly, without hypocrisy, standing open and transparent before Him.

ANNE GRAHAM LOTZ

Your Partnership with God

For we are God's co-workers. You are God's field, God's building.

1 Corinthians 3:9 HCSB

Do you seek a life of purpose, abundance, and fulfillment? If so, then you must form a partnership with God.

You are God's work-in-progress. God wants to mold your heart and guide your path, but because He created you as a creature of free will, He will not force you to become His. That choice is yours alone, and it is a choice that should be reflected in every decision you make and every step you take.

Today, as you encounter the challenges of everyday life, strengthen your partnership with God through prayer, through obedience, through praise, through thanksgiving, and through service. God is the ultimate partner, and He wants to be your partner in every aspect of your life. Please don't turn Him down.

When you invite God to become your partner, you invite untold blessings into your life.

Marie T. Freeman

Honoring God

Honor the Lord with your possessions, and with the firstfruits of all your increase; so your barns will be filled with plenty.

PROVERBS 3:9-10 NKJV

Whom will you choose to honor today? If you honor God and place Him at the center of your life, every day is a cause for celebration. But if you fail to honor your Heavenly Father, you're asking for trouble, and lots of it.

At times, your life is probably hectic, demanding, and complicated. When the demands of life leave you rushing from place to place with scarcely a moment to spare, you may fail to pause and thank your Creator for the blessings He has bestowed upon you. But that's a big mistake.

Do you sincerely seek to be a worthy servant of the One who has given you eternal love and eternal life? Then honor Him for who He is and for what He has done for you. And don't just honor Him on Sunday morning. Praise Him all day long, every day, for as long as you live . . . and then for all eternity.

Acceptance Today

I have learned to be content whatever the circumstances.
PHILIPPIANS 4:11 NIV

Are you embittered by a personal tragedy that you did not deserve and cannot understand? If so, it's time to accept the unchangeable past and to have faith in the promise of tomorrow. It's time to trust God completely—and it's time to reclaim the peace—His peace—that can and should be yours.

On occasion, you will be confronted with situations that you simply don't understand. But God does. And He has a reason for everything that He does.

God doesn't explain Himself in ways that we, as mortals with limited insight and clouded vision, can comprehend. So, instead of understanding every aspect of God's unfolding plan for our lives and our universe, we must be satisfied to trust Him completely. We cannot know God's motivations, nor can we understand His actions. We can, however, trust Him, and we must.

I have held many things in my hands, and I have lost them all; but whatever I have placed in God's hands, that I still possess.

CORRIE TEN BOOM

Talking to the Father

You do not have because you do not ask.

JAMES 4:2 HCSB

Sometimes, amid the demands and the frustrations of everyday life, we forget to slow ourselves down long enough to talk with God. Instead of turning our thoughts and prayers to Him, we rely upon our own resources. Instead of praying for strength and courage, we seek to manufacture it within ourselves. Instead of asking God for guidance, we depend only upon our own limited wisdom. The results of such behaviors are unfortunate and, on occasion, tragic.

Are you in need? Ask God to sustain you. Are you troubled? Take your worries to Him in prayer. Are you weary? Seek God's strength. In all things great and small, seek God's wisdom and His grace. He hears your prayers, and He will answer. All you must do is ask.

God will help us become the people we are meant to be, if only we will ask Him.

HANNAH WHITALL SMITH

When you ask God to do something, don't ask timidly; put your whole heart into it.

MARIE T. FREEMAN

Each Day a Gift

Shout triumphantly to the Lord, all the earth. Serve the Lord with gladness; come before Him with joyful songs.
PSALM 100:1-2 HCSB

Life should never be taken for granted. Each day is a priceless gift from God and should be treated as such.

Hannah Whitall Smith observed, "How changed our lives would be if we could only fly through the days on wings of surrender and trust!" And Clement of Alexandria noted, "All our life is a celebration for us; we are convinced, in fact, that God is always everywhere. We sing while we work . . . we pray while we carry out all life's other occupations." These words remind us that this day is God's creation, a gift to be treasured and savored.

Today, let us celebrate life with smiles on our faces and kind words on our lips. After all, this is God's day, and He has given us clear instructions for its use. We are commanded to rejoice and be glad. So, with no further ado, let the celebration begin . . .

Morning praise will make your days.

ANONYMOUS

Christ's Love

Just as the Father has loved Me, I also have loved you.
Remain in My love.

JOHN 15:9 HCSB

How much does Christ love us? More than we, as mere mortals, can comprehend. His love is perfect and steadfast. Even though we are fallible and wayward, the Good Shepherd cares for us still. Even though we have fallen far short of the Father's commandments, Christ loves us with a power and depth that is beyond our understanding. The sacrifice that Jesus made upon the cross was made for each of us, and His love endures to the edge of eternity and beyond.

Christ's love changes everything. When you accept His gift of grace, you are transformed, not only for today, but also for all eternity. If you haven't already done so, accept Jesus Christ as your Savior. He's waiting patiently for you to invite Him into your heart. Please don't make Him wait a single minute longer.

We are the earthen vessels, the jars of clay, that bring the life and love of Christ to one another.

SHEILA WALSH

Your Daily Journey

Then He said to them all, "If anyone wants to come with Me, he must deny himself, take up his cross daily, and follow Me."

LUKE 9:23 HCSB

Even the most inspired women can, from time to time, find themselves running on empty. Why? Because the inevitable demands of daily life can drain us of our strength and rob us of the joy that is rightfully ours in Christ. Thankfully, God stands ready to renew our spirits, even on the darkest of days. God's Word is clear: When we genuinely lift our hearts and prayers to Him, He renews our strength.

Are you almost too weary to lift your head? Then bow it—in prayer. Offer your concerns and your needs to your Father in heaven. He is always at your side, offering His love and His strength.

Your search to discover God's purpose for your life is not a destination; it is a journey that unfolds day by day. And, that's exactly how often you should seek direction from your Creator: one day at a time, each day followed by the next, without exception.

The Power of Encouragement

*He comes alongside us when we go through hard times,
and before you know it, he brings us alongside someone
else who is going through hard times so that we can be
there for that person just as God was there for us.*

2 CORINTHIANS 1:4 MSG

Do you delight in the victories of others? You should. Each day provides countless opportunities to encourage others and to praise their good works. When you do so, you spread seeds of joy and happiness.

American poet Ella Wheeler Wilcox advised, "Talk happiness. The world is sad enough without your woe." Her words still apply.

Life is a team sport, and all of us need occasional pats on the back from our teammates. So, let us be cheerful with smiles on our faces and encouraging words on our lips. By blessing others, we also bless ourselves, and, when we do, God smiles.

One of the ways God refills us after failure is through the blessing of Christian fellowship. Just experiencing the joy of simple activities shared with other children of God can have a healing effect on us.

ANNE GRAHAM LOTZ

No Excuses

Let us live in a right way . . . clothe yourselves with the Lord Jesus Christ and forget about satisfying your sinful self.

ROMANS 13:13-14 NCV

Excuses are everywhere . . . excellence is not. Whether you're a stay-at-home mom or a corporate CEO, your work is a picture book of your priorities. So whatever your job description, it's up to you, and no one else, to become masterful at your craft. It's up to you to do your job right, and to do it right now.

Because we humans are such creative excuse-makers, all of the best excuses have already been taken—we've heard them all before.

So if you're wasting your time trying to concoct a new and improved excuse, don't bother. It's impossible. A far better strategy is this: do the work. Now. Then, let your excellent work speak loudly and convincingly for itself.

Never use your problem as an excuse for bad attitudes or behavior.

JOYCE MEYER

Follow Him

If anyone serves Me, let him follow Me; and where I am, there My servant will be also. If anyone serves Me, him My Father will honor.

JOHN 12:26 NKJV

Jesus walks with you. Are you walking with Him? Hopefully, you will choose to walk with Him today and every day of your life.

Jesus loved you so much that He endured unspeakable humiliation and suffering for you. How will you respond to Christ's sacrifice? Will you take up His cross and follow Him (Luke 9:23) or will you choose another path? When you place your hopes squarely at the foot of the cross, when you place Jesus squarely at the center of your life, you will be blessed. If you seek to be a worthy disciple of Jesus, you must acknowledge that He never comes "next." He is always first.

Do you hope to fulfill God's purpose for your life? Do you seek a life of abundance and peace? Do you intend to be a Christian, not just in name, but in deed? Then follow Christ. Follow Him by picking up His cross today and every day that you live. When you do, you will quickly discover that Christ's love has the power to change everything, including you.

Your Very Bright Future

For I know the thoughts that I think toward you, says the Lord, thoughts of peace and not of evil, to give you a future and a hope. Then you will call upon Me and go and pray to Me, and I will listen to you.

JEREMIAH 29:11-12 NKJV

How bright is your future? The answer, in all likelihood, is that your future is so bright that you'd better wear shades!

Now, here's something else to ponder: How bright do you believe your future to be? Are you expecting a terrific tomorrow, or are you dreading a terrible one? And make no mistake: the answer to this second set of questions will have a powerful impact on the way tomorrow turns out.

Corrie ten Boom had this advice: "Never be afraid to trust an unknown future to a known God." And it's advice that most certainly applies to you. So, with no further ado, it's time to trust God . . . and put on the shades.

For Christians who believe God's promises, the future is actually too bright to comprehend.

MARIE T. FREEMAN

Heeding His Call

I, therefore, the prisoner in the Lord, urge you to walk worthy of the calling you have received.

EPHESIANS 4:1 HCSB

It is terribly important that you heed God's calling by discovering and developing your talents and your spiritual gifts. If you seek to make a difference—and if you seek to bear eternal fruit—you must discover your gifts and begin using them for the glory of God.

Every believer has at least one gift. In John 15:16, Jesus says, "You did not choose Me, but I chose you and appointed you that you should go and bear fruit, and that your fruit should remain, that whatever you ask the Father in My name He may give you." Have you found your special calling? If not, keep searching and keep praying until you find it. God has important work for you to do, and the time to begin that work is now.

If God has called you, do not spend time looking over your shoulder to see who is following you.

CORRIE TEN BOOM

God never calls without enabling us. In other words, if he calls you to do something, he makes it possible for you to do it.

LUCI SWINDOLL

Finding His Love

He has not stopped showing his kindness to the living and the dead . . . .

RUTH 2:20 NIV

Where can we find God's love? Everywhere. God's love transcends space and time. It reaches beyond the heavens, and it touches the darkest, smallest corner of every human heart. When we sincerely open our minds and hearts to God, His love does not arrive "some day"—it arrives immediately.

Joyce Meyer reminds us that, "God has the marvelous ability to love us in the midst of our imperfections." And if He can love us unconditionally, we should find the wisdom and the courage to love ourselves, come what may.

So today, take God at His word and welcome His love into your heart. When you do, God's transcendent love will surround you and transform you, now and always.

When you invite the love of God into your heart, everything in the world looks different, including you.

MARIE T. FREEMAN

He Is By Your Side

*I have set the Lord always before me; because He is at my
right hand I shall not be moved.*

PSALM 16:8 NKJV

God loves us and protects us. In times of trouble,
He comforts us; in times of sorrow, He dries our
tears. Psalm 147 promises, "He heals the brokenhearted,
and binds their wounds" (v. 3, NASB). When we are
troubled, we must call upon God, and—in His own
time and according to His own plan—He will heal us.

Do you feel fearful, or weak, or sorrowful? Are you
discouraged or bitter? Do you feel "stuck" in a place
that is uncomfortable for you? If so, remember that
God is as near as your next breath. So trust Him and
turn to Him for solace, for security, and for salvation.
And build your life on the rock that cannot be shaken
. . . that rock is God.

God promises us a safe landing, not smooth sailing.

ANONYMOUS

Worries carry responsibilities that belong to God, not
to you. Worry does not enable us to escape evil; it makes
us unfit to cope with it when it comes.

CORRIE TEN BOOM

His Plan

The steps of the Godly are directed by the Lord. He delights in every detail of their lives. Though they stumble, they will not fall, for the Lord holds them by the hand.

PSALM 37:23-24 NLT

God has a plan for our world and for our lives—He does not do things by accident. God is willful and intentional, but we cannot always understand His purposes. Why? Because we are mortal beings with limited understanding. And although we cannot fully comprehend the will of God, we should always trust the will of God.

As this day unfolds, seek God's will and obey His Word. When you entrust your life to Him without reservation, He will give you the courage meet any challenge, the strength to endure any trial, and the wisdom to live in His righteousness and in His peace.

In the Garden of Gethsemane, Jesus went through agony of soul in His efforts to resist the temptation to do what He felt like doing rather than what He knew was God's will for Him.

JOYCE MEYER

Eternally Grateful and Exceedingly Humble

God is against the proud, but he gives grace to the humble.

1 PETER 5:5 NCV

God's Word clearly instructs us to be humble. And that's good because, as fallible human beings, we have so very much to be humble about! Yet some of us continue to puff ourselves up, seeming to say, "Look at me!" To do so is wrong.

As Christians, we have been refashioned and saved by Jesus Christ, and that salvation came not because of our own good works but because of God's grace. How, then, can we be prideful? The answer, of course, is that, if we are honest with ourselves and with our God, we simply can't be boastful . . . we must, instead, be eternally grateful and exceedingly humble. The good things in our lives, including our loved ones, come from God. He deserves the credit—and we deserve the glorious experience of giving it to Him.

The gate of heaven is very low; only the humble can enter it.

ELIZABETH ANN SETON

The Gift of Laughter

Clap your hands, all you nations; shout to God with cries of joy.

PSALM 47:1 NIV

Laughter is a gift from God, a gift that He intends for us to use. Yet sometimes, because of the inevitable stresses of everyday living, we fail to find the fun in life. When we allow life's inevitable disappointments to cast a pall over our lives and our souls, we do a profound disservice to ourselves and to our loved ones.

As Christians we have every reason to be cheerful and to be thankful. Our blessings from God are beyond measure, starting, of course, with a gift that is ours for the asking, God's gift of salvation through Christ Jesus.

Few things in life are more absurd than the sight of a grumpy, sour-faced Christian. So today, as you go about your daily activities, approach life with a smile and a chuckle. After all, God created laughter for a reason . . . and Father indeed knows best. So laugh!

Laughter dulls the sharpest pain and flattens out the greatest stress. To share it is to give a gift of health.

BARBARA JOHNSON